FOUNDATIONS OF
A CATHOLIC POLITICAL ORDER

Foundations
of a
Catholic
Political Order

Second Edition

THOMAS STORCK

Foreword by
Peter A. Kwasniewski

AROUCA
PRESS

978-1-989905-96-8 (pbk)
978-1-989905-97-5 (hardcover)

Arouca Press
PO Box 55003
Bridgeport PO
Waterloo, ON N2J 3G0
Canada
www.aroucapress.com
Send inquiries to info@aroucapress.com

To my wife
Mulieris bonae beatus vir
numerus enim annorum illius duplex.
—Sirach 26:1

"So long as Christ does not reign over nations, His influence over individuals remains superficial and precarious. If it is true that the work of the apostolate consists in the conversion of individuals and that nations as such do not go to Heaven, but souls, one by one, we must not forget, nevertheless, that the individual member of society lives under the never-ceasing influence of his environment, in which, if we may not say that he is submerged, he is, at least, deeply plunged. If the environment is non-Catholic, it prevents him from embracing the faith, or if he has the faith, it tends to root out of his heart every vestige of belief. If we imagine Catholic social institutions, with Our Lord no longer living in the hearts of the individual members of society, then religion has there become a displeasing signboard which will soon be torn down. But, on the other hand, try to convert individuals without Catholicizing the social institutions and your work is without stability. The structure you erect in the morning will be torn down by others in the evening. Is not the strategy of the enemies of God there to teach us a lesson? They want to destroy the faith in the hearts of individuals, it is true, but they direct still more vigorous efforts to the elimination of religion from social institutions. Even one defeat of God in this domain means the weakening, if not the ruin, of the faith in the souls of many."

—Louis Cardinal Pie (1815–1880)

CONTENTS

THE POLITICAL DIMENSION
OF THE CHURCH'S
SOCIAL MAGISTERIUM

NUMEROUS ARE THE STUDIES WRITTEN on the social Magisterium of the Church. What makes Thomas Storck's *Foundations of a Catholic Political Order* stand out from the rest of them is the welcome and striking attention he pays to the specifically political elements and ramifications of this body of doctrine, which are often sidelined by an almost exclusive focus on economics and "trendy" topics like race, immigration, low-income housing, and the like. None of these topics is without its importance, but to most people it must seem as if Catholic Social Teaching (CST) is nothing more than a hodge-podge of idealistic exhortations on a miscellany of subjects. The value of the present work consists in its provision of a more comprehensive and coherent framework for CST and a better interpretation of its basic consistency over the past several centuries, together with a needed correction of longstanding errors in the field.

The author's pervasive concern is announced at the start in a quotation from Cardinal Pie: "So long as Christ does not reign over nations, His influence over individuals remains superficial and precarious." *Foundations* is an extended reflection on the relationship between how a society is ordered in its cultural-political institutions and how the Catholic faith is internalized by individual believers. In the words of

Glen Olsen: "A full Christian life is one lived out in one's art, one's politics, the form one's city takes, and any check placed on public expression of one's Christianity is an attack on the possibility of living an integrated life, an attempt to disallow Christian maturation." In the modern world (or at least in the modern West), it is often assumed without question that religion is a strictly private matter and that the only things which ought to exist in the public domain are the supposedly neutral activities of running the government and conducting commerce. Yet this assumption, and the very terms in which it is expressed, are part of a secular dogmatic creed we have inherited from the Enlightenment. Why do we unquestioningly accept an institutionalized dichotomy between the religious and the secular, the sacred and the profane, when this state of affairs is a deeply unnatural contradiction and would have been recognized as such at any other time in the history of nations and peoples? Upon closer investigation, "the most basic constituent of a culture, the one that shapes it throughout, is its theological orientation, its religion or its secular substitute for religion," writes Storck. In this conviction Storck unites with other modern political thinkers such as Pierre Manent, Alisdair MacIntyre, William Cavanaugh, Edmund Waldstein, and Thaddeus Kozinski.

Storck approaches from an openly political angle a perennial issue addressed many times by the popes, namely, the extent to which faith and culture should intertwine, mutually supporting one another: "I develop the political and juridical aspects of such a [Catholic] culture, that is, those formal political and juridical institutions, in their most general aspects, which seem to me necessary for the preservation, stability and perfection of a Catholic culture." Catholicism is an intrinsically *social* religion that permeates and transforms from within every aspect of life and culture. "A faith that does not become culture," said John Paul II, "would be a faith not fully received, not entirely thought out, and not faithfully lived." On the basis of this truth, Storck goes on to show that only a Catholic political order can fully safeguard a Catholic culture, thus introducing his plan for the rest of the work: "I will take up what this role of protecting and perfecting a Catholic culture might actually look like. What would be the powers and duties of a Catholic state, what special institutions might it have or foster, what would be the spirit of its approach to governing?"

The jaundiced post-conciliar reader might wonder if the Church herself really puts forward the possibility and desirability of a Catholic political order in her official teachings, if she actually embraces the positive interaction of the political and religious domains. Storck's answer is a firm yes and his supporting evidence is plentiful. The Church *does* have political principles to teach us, and her doctrine in this area is no less a part of her universal ordinary Magisterium than teachings on, for example, economic or conjugal morality. Combining quotations from political philosophers and official Church documents with his own commentary, Storck unfolds the *integral* social wisdom of the Catholic Faith. He brings into focus manifest contradictions between what the Church teaches and what the Western world — including, alas, many a self-appointed authority on Catholic social doctrine — condones and practices today. Throughout, the author rightly opposes the all-too-common reduction of the Church's social Magisterium to a limited body of suggestions on purely economic matters. We have been trained to equate the social Magisterium with the economic dimension of *Rerum Novarum*, *Quadragesimo Anno*, and *Centesimus Annus*, forgetting, first, that these encyclicals contain far more than recommendations for redressing economic injustice, and, secondly, that they constitute only a fraction of what the Church has taught about social issues in all their amplitude, such as the solemn responsibilities of secular states towards the true religion, the absolute obligation of the state to uphold marriage and sustain the irreplaceable work of the family, the right of parents to educate their own children as they see fit, or the essentially *public* nature of worship and religious profession.

As part of our heritage of miseducation, Catholics have been led to believe that the American compromise, where religion and the political sphere have (formally speaking) little or nothing to do with one another, is normative, whereas in fact the Church teaches the opposite. A generation of theologians from the last century, led by John Courtney Murray, continued the nineteenth-century liberal attempt to bring the Church's teaching into line with Americanism. In the process, the rich and nuanced teaching of the Church suffered a terrible distortion. As a result, most treatments of CST to this day reflect with greater accuracy the fantasies of these latter-day Americanists than the actual declarations issued by popes and Councils. In all of this, we can see a pattern of deliberately reducing all political issues to economic ones, and a corresponding tendency to pretend that the Church has renounced the political ideals she once defended. Americans treasure the rights of freedom of speech, press, and conscience; the constitutional separation of church and state; a free-market system of liberal capitalism based on international banking and interest-levying; and, most sacrosanct of all, the principle of popular sovereignty or the consent of the governed, which finds the root of political authority in the will of the people, from whom all secular power is believed to emanate. Underlying the popular account of these freedoms, this economic infrastructure, the divorce of spiritual and temporal powers, and above all the social contract theory frequently invoked by the American founding fathers is a philosophy condemned by the Supreme Pontiffs of the Church in so clear and authoritative a manner that any reversal of doctrine in this area is impossible.

The Church's statements on modern political theory span from the first warnings of Pius VI in 1775 to the powerful proclamations of Leo XIII and his successors to an encyclical like John Paul II's *Evangelium Vitae*, which contains a frontal attack on the Enlightenment understanding of man and human society (cf. nn. 18–23, 69–70). In the eyes of the Church, the philosophical principles of government enshrined in modern regimes are antithetical to the Faith, contrary to human nature, and destructive of the common good of society. In *Aeterni Patris*, to take one example among many, Pope Leo XIII writes: "Whosoever turns his attention to the bitter strifes of these days and seeks a reason for the troubles that vex public and private life must come to the conclusion that a fruitful cause of the evils which now afflict, as well as those which threaten us, lies in this: that false conclusions concerning divine and human things, which originated in the schools of philosophy, have crept into all the orders of the state, and have been accepted by the common consent of the masses" (n. 2). While not intended as a response to Americanism *per se*, Storck's book presents a fresh and compelling critique of its philosophical assumptions and a corresponding exposition of the Church's doctrine concerning the proper conception of the political order.

In presenting an overview of what the Church has taught and what reason approves regarding such matters as religious liberty, economic activity, censorship, family law, and democracy, Storck returns frequently to the notion of the "normative situation," namely, a Catholic cultural environment fostered and protected by a Catholic political order. According to the mind of the Church, this situation is the *norm* in all senses. It arises naturally when the Faith is not impeded by hostile forces; it is eminently desirable among those who profess the Faith from their hearts; and it is the standard against which existing systems are to be judged. The normative situation comes into being when a Catholic population, guided by the spirit of the Gospel and prompted by the inner logic of the Faith, develops a unified life woven of the separate strands of religion, art, education, government, leisure, recreation, allowing "the full and free expression and flowering of Catholicism." Among such a people, there is no practical schizophrenia, no division between what is professed as eternally true and what is lived from day to day. Small things of daily importance reflect and reinforce things of supernatural and everlasting importance; sublime realities of the Faith are given space and freedom to mold the activities of ordinary life, sanctifying them in the process. It is only in this way, in fact, that human society *justifies* its own existence after the coming of Christ. The worth of a society, as of any government or political system, is measured by one standard only, which is at the same time the most truly humanistic or man-perfecting concern: eternal salvation. Does a society with its political and economic structures on the whole advance or retard the gaining of everlasting life in Christ? This is the final measure for judging the political structures man has built, and this alone should be the Catholic's mindset when distinguishing what is praiseworthy from what is merely tolerable or worthy of condemnation and even, at times, of organized resistance.

Wherever the Faith is preached with full conviction, the ultimate goal can be no other than the conversion of human nature in its *totality* by the truth of revelation and the power of grace. "The normal practice of the Catholic faith encourages or even requires community among its adherents, and will transform its external environment to reflect that community and its Faith; in other words, it will create a culture," our author explains. "If it is true that Catholicism in its normal state will flourish in a thousand practices and will thoroughly hallow a culture, and that this is the natural effect of the living Faith, then it follows that the natural state of a Catholic is to live in a Catholic culture, the only place where Catholic life can be lived as it ought to be lived." A Catholic culture develops common practices: "numerous public and common celebrations and activities, institutions and organizations, in which the Faith is publicly expressed and works carried on to further some object, spiritual or temporal, connected with the Faith." To wit:

> In addition to sacramental and other rituals, either in or outside the church building itself, there are numerous sodalities and confraternities, processions, pilgrimages, observances of feast days with popular devotions and other traditions such as dramas, dances, games or sports, not to mention activities to relieve or otherwise aid the poor, including charitable establishments of many kinds, cooperatives and special funds for needs, such as dowries for poor girls. Catholicism has also hallowed many of the everyday pursuits of mankind, with blessings of houses, land, fishing fleets, tools, food and drink and numerous other items and tasks.

If unity of faith and life is the positive reason for the desirability of Catholic culture, there is a negative one, too: "the protection of the individual believer from error and sin." Such a culture "helps him to remember to dedicate his whole being and life and work to God." It is man's fallen condition, the bitter harvest of original sin, that makes it obligatory for a properly constituted civil authority to *restrain* human beings from vicious acts. If men are born into the world with a tendency towards evil—a far cry from Rousseau's fantasy of the noble savage—they stand in need of as many corrective influences as possible. The family and the state, as the two most potent forces on the individual, stand under a divine obligation to shape the soul in virtue and arm it against vice. If the individual grows up with a non-religious family life and the systematic anti-religious indoctrination typical of most of our modern schools, there can be no humanly reasonable expectation that the effects of original sin will be addressed and mitigated. On the contrary, such effects will flourish and multiply and, like a virus, develop ever new variants of perversity. It is frightening, then, to ponder this remark by the intellectual historian Ernst Cassirer: "The concept of original sin is the common opponent against which all the different trends of the philosophy of the Enlightenment join forces."[1] The widespread attitude that a person should be able to do whatever he or she wants, provided it "does no harm to anyone else," and that the state has nothing to do with promoting Christian morality or belief, is rooted in a dual rejection of man's fallen condition and of his supernatural vocation. Those who profess the Faith, with its promise of liberating the mind as well as the heart, must come to recognize and reject the Enlightenment ideology that has turned the contemporary Western world into a chaos of nihilistic materialism that recognizes no higher law than self-will.

Not one to dodge a challenge, Storck devotes the second chapter, and a more detailed appendix, to a consideration of what might seem an insuperable objection to his entire

---

1 *The Philosophy of the Enlightenment*, trans. Fritz C. A. Koelln and James P. Pettegrove (Boston: Beacon Press, 1955), 141.

enterprise: the purported teaching of *Dignitatis Humanae*, the decree on religious liberty of the Second Vatican Council. It does not require much familiarity with the Church to know that there are Catholics for whom the mere title of this conciliar document functions like a magic spell against everything Storck's book seeks to establish. I find Storck's effort to make the document intelligible and defensible *in light of* that traditional teaching a serious and worthwhile endeavor that, at very least, dismisses simplistic readings. In the appendix, Thomas Storck critiques Thomas Pink's reading of *Dignitatis Humanae*, which has acquired a substantial following in recent years.[2]

In chapter 3, "The Framework of Economic Activity," Storck places the limited theories and activities of economics in a larger context, namely, that of the common good to be achieved in the political community as a whole, showing that the common good is certainly far more than the acquisition of wealth, gross national product, low unemployment, or equal distribution of material goods. Economics of its very nature must be subordinated to the common good; it certainly cannot produce that good by itself. Storck delves into the nature of free enterprise, the parameters of commerce and advertising, the necessity of a structure of subsidiary economic groups, the evils associated with banking based on the levying of interest, and alternatives to the dominant economic models of the West. Chapter 4, "Censorship," briefly considers how and why the Catholic state must wisely use means of restricting and channeling the various media of information with a view to fostering the common good. In our era of

---

2   Pink has written a response: "On *Dignitatis Humanae*—A Reply to Thomas Storck," published online at *The Josias* on October 28, 2021. Storck then responded: "What Did *Dignitatis Humanae* Do? A Reply to Thomas Pink," available at academia.edu.

addictive and destructive pornography that routinely exploits women and children and causes permanent psychological injury, his message here would be difficult to disagree with. Chapter 5, "Family Law and Other Legal Matters," displays the author's grasp of concrete detail and his solid common sense. Using the Charter of Family Rights from *Familiaris Consortio*, Storck explains how these rights are under siege not only by the laws and policies of current regimes but by the very philosophy on which the modern state is based. He then outlines ways in which a society ruled in accordance with CST could successfully meet the difficulties of our times in regard, for instance, to marriage, welfare, housing, ecology, labor laws, education, and technology. Storck's indictment of the serious evils engendered by certain forms of technology and capitalist models of production offers a healthy corrective to the blind veneration of our age's industrial-economic accomplishments. Chapter 6, "Democracy," sketches the kind of social structures most supportive of a genuine culture, such as the blending of democratic and aristocratic modes of rulership and the necessity of intermediate entities, like occupational groups and cooperatives, endowed with political representation.

The last chapter, "The Ultimate Preservatives of a Christian Culture," takes up the question of "what, in the long run, must be hoped for to preserve a Catholic culture in all its vitality and vibrant orthodoxy." No Christian culture has, of itself, the capacity for perpetual life; the resplendent Catholic culture of Europe has tragically declined until it is now barely a memory. Storck counsels: "It is certainly also right for us to learn from what happened before and, as much as we can, provide effective safeguards for the future — if there is any future for a Catholic state and Catholic culture." Storck focuses the question: "Is there anything which can protect a

Catholic culture *from within*, as it were, anything which we can foster which will make it more probable that a Christian civilization will stand against the decline in faith and fervor and charity that too often afflicts Catholics?" His answer: we must renew serious Catholic intellectual formation and cultivate a strong interior life of faith, hope, and charity. Only in these two ways can we slowly restore the Catholic culture needed for the full flowering of our holy religion. Here it is not amiss to point out that history shows us the surprising rapidity with which declining and self-sabotaging civilizations can collapse as younger and stronger cultural forces enter in. God alone knows the future, which lies in His hands, and which He will bring about by the use of secondary causes that are or may seem, in themselves, to be totally disproportionate to the goal He has in mind. The conquest of the ancient world by the Catholic Faith is, of course, the abiding example. We cannot and must not resign ourselves to an attitude of defeatism and despair, but do what is good and right and holy, and leave the rest to Providence. The Lord has, after all, made the world from nothing, transformed water into wine, and fed thousands from a few loaves and fishes.

Storck's apt citations of classic and modern authors (among them Aristotle, St. Thomas Aquinas, Dawson, Belloc, Tawney, Fanfani, Pieper, Ratzinger, and Giussani), his references to specialized studies in economics and political science, and his impressive command of magisterial documents make *Foundations of a Catholic Political Order* a provocative challenge to the conventional soft-pedaling of Catholic political teaching. It will therefore be a very great disappointment, and possibly a cause of apoplexy, to those who, whether "liberal" or "conservative," cherish the belief that modern political philosophy or modern political systems are, at root, compatible with Catholicism. In point of fact, it is probably impossible to find two visions of reality that are more opposed than these, and if one wishes to be consistent with oneself, one must ultimately choose between them, however long one must labor in the blighted vineyards while looking to the city shining on the hill. Storck has written a book that bears witness to the maximizing demands of the Faith in its relation to the world. Christ came to save not just individuals but societies as well. Everything natural is included in the scope of His salvific power; everything human is intended, by divine Providence, to be sanctified and ordered to our final home, the City of God in heaven. May Storck's book help to renew a discussion too long silenced and a Christian way of life too long dormant.

Peter A. Kwasniewski
December 17, 2021
Ember Friday of Advent

PREFACE TO THE
SECOND EDITION

THE FIRST EDITION OF THIS BOOK
appeared in 1998. At that time there was comparatively little
discussion in the Catholic world, at least in the United States,
of the Church's traditional teaching on the duty of the state
to render honor to God, and the bearing of this teaching
on the question of religious freedom for non-Catholics in a
Catholic state, and even less of what might be the contours
of a Catholic political order. But much has changed since
then, in fact, the incompatibility of the Catholic faith and the
liberal political system which has reigned for so long in the
Western world is being increasingly recognized. Catholics are
finally taking seriously the teaching of Leo XIII, a teaching
that was often ignored or downplayed in this country well
before the Second Vatican Council.

For several years I had contemplated a revised edition of
this book. Because of the increasing interest in the question
of the political implications of the Faith, the terms of the
debate over religious liberty and the decree of the Second
Vatican Council, *Dignitatis Humanae*, have changed. The
two books which I discussed at length in the first edition,
in Appendix II, Fr. Brian Harrison's *Religious Liberty and
Contraception* and Mr. Michael Davies' *The Second Vatican
Council and Religious Liberty*, no longer are at the crux of
the debate over *Dignitatis Humanae*, so it seemed best to
include a new Appendix II devoted to more current contro-
versies over *Dignitatis Humanae*. I have omitted the original
Appendix I, a somewhat fanciful description of a mythical

Catholic state, not by way of necessarily repudiating anything in it, but because I felt that it unnecessarily linked the general themes of this book to too specific a suggested application. A new Appendix I deals with similarities and differences between distributism and solidarism as Catholic approaches to organizing an economy.

The introductory chapter needed significant revision in order to show more clearly that a regime that honors our Lord as King is demanded not only as a protection for a Catholic culture but by the very nature of such a *polis*. Initially I did not think that the remaining chapters required a thorough rewriting, but in reviewing the text I found more that in my judgment needed to be revised than I expected, and so I have made more or less extensive changes to those as well.

I fear that this book will appear to some readers as an exercise in utter unreality. The present state of the Church, let alone of what remains of Catholic cultures, hardly suggests that any time soon we will be establishing new Catholic states. All that I admit, and, speaking for myself, I incline much more to the view that "the times of the Gentiles" (Luke 21:24) are about at their end, rather than that we should expect some extraordinary revival of the Faith. If so, it is the sober words of our Lord, "Nevertheless, when the Son of man comes, will he find faith on earth?" (Luke 18:8), to which we must attend, rather than to prophecies of revival. However, this does not mean that it is useless to think about what the outlines of a Catholic state might be. If we are becoming more aware that the Faith is not compatible with the liberal social order of the last few centuries, then what would we want to replace it with? What might a Catholic social order look like at the present day? It is one thing to criticize the present political and cultural situation, it is another thing to propose something to replace it. And it seems to me that part of setting our thinking in order is to know what we have in mind, or might have in mind, to put in place of the present liberal order.

The impetus for my finally revising this book came from Mr. Luiz de Moraes of the Instituto Santo Atanásio in Brazil who approached me late last year for permission to translate this work into Portuguese. At the time I was unable to completely revise the book, but I did rewrite the introductory chapter and included the revised Appendix II on religious liberty. I am grateful to him for being the catalyst for my undertaking the work of revision.

I also wish to thank those who gave the first edition a warm reception, particularly Dr. Peter Kwasniewski and Dr. David Arias, Jr.

Thomas Storck
Transfiguration of Our Lord, 2021

*   *   *

There are a great many quotations from papal encyclicals, other ecclesiastical documents, and certain civil legal texts in this book, and in the first edition I noted the sources for the various translations or editions I used. This seems less necessary in this edition, since translations of probably all of the documents I cite are available online, and these online sources are more readily available to readers than the printed compilations I used, which are mostly out of print. The official text (usually Latin) of most Church documents appears in the *Acta Apostolicae Sedis*, and generally the Vatican website will contain the Latin text as well as translations into several languages. But there are no official translations of older ecclesiastical texts, and for the most part the English translations on the Vatican website of these older documents are taken from previously published private translations. Another point to be noted, is that the Latin text of older documents did not have numbered paragraphs. These have frequently been added by translators, but different translators have made different divisions of the text. A further difficulty is that the section or paragraph numbering of documents on the Vatican website differs in various languages, and sometimes the Latin text (when available) does not have numbered paragraphs at all.

PREFACE TO FIRST EDITION

THIS BOOK IS INTENDED TO BE A CON-
tinuation of the general theme I first treated of in my 1987
book, *The Catholic Milieu*, which dealt with the culture of
a Catholic civilization. In this present work I develop the
political and juridical aspects of such a culture, that is, those
formal political and juridical institutions, in their most general aspects, which seem to me necessary for the preservation,
stability and perfection of a Catholic culture. Because this
connection between Catholicism and the political order will
strike many as novel, I think it might be well to say a few
words about this here.

I have noticed in the last few years a growing awareness on
the part of Catholics of the necessity for what can be called
Catholic culture, that is, we are becoming aware that Catholicism is not an individualistic religion. The Faith transforms
not only individual lives but societies. The Faith creates a
social order and does this on every level of culture. And
as Catholics devote more attention to this fact, sooner or
later we are going to have to face up to the question of the
political order. Can the political order likewise be brought
into subjection to Christ the King? Or is it somehow outside
any possibility of being baptized? Our tradition, of course, is
clear on this matter: the state can be christianized. Catholic
teaching long ago consecrated the notion of the Catholic
state, and Catholic practice, however imperfectly, attempted
to make that teaching a reality. In doing so, as I will argue,
we were simply facing up to the fact that man organized on a
political level is as much in need of God as man organized in

any other way. When we realize this, then we can begin thinking seriously about what form a Catholic state might take.

Catholics in America have rarely been comfortable with such an inquiry, however. We have generally been satisfied, even happy, with our constitutional arrangements toward church and state. But as long ago as 1895 Pope Leo XIII felt called upon to remind us that, however prosperous the condition of the Church was in the U. S., "it would be very erroneous to draw the conclusion that in America is to be sought the type of the most desirable status of the Church" or that the separation of Church and state was "universally lawful or expedient." Moreover, he stated that the Church in this country "would bring forth more abundant fruits if, in addition to liberty, she enjoyed the favor of the laws and the patronage of the public authority" (Encyclical *Longinqua Oceani*, January 6, 1895). And because of what I consider widespread misunderstandings of what the Second Vatican Council really taught, it has become even harder to find a sympathetic audience for this traditional teaching than it was a century ago.

The question of a Catholic state should, it seems to me, be regarded as an aspect of the question of the sanctification of culture. That is, if we realize the necessity, even inevitability, of the Faith influencing the external and public life of Catholics, then the question of the political order becomes inescapable. Only considered in this way will the arguments in this book make sense. For if we approach the question of a Catholic state simply and primarily as a political question, not only will we be committing an intellectual error, but we will be stirring up all the bitterness that political questions too often give rise to. For the Catholic state is ultimately rooted in the faith and holiness of individual Catholics, and in the faith and holiness that we naturally seek to create in the world around us.

It is true, of course, that today not only are there no Catholic states in existence, but there is no prospect for the establishment of any. But nonetheless I do not think that an attempt to explore this question is useless, and that for two reasons. First, an attempt to delineate truths, no matter how far from a foreseeable application, is never vain, since it is never vain to set our thinking in order; and second, it may be that in future centuries Catholic cultures and Catholic states will again become realities, and thus our thinking about what they should be like may perhaps make some small contribution to the work of our descendants in the Faith.

To many outside the Church, no doubt it seems that now is hardly the time to be planning for future Catholic civilizations, for as far as they can see, not only is Catholic culture dead, but the Catholic Church herself is in an irreversible decline. For them our discussion of this subject may be likened to the action of those Romans who so irritated Hannibal. After defeating nearly every Roman army sent against him, Hannibal was finally encamped in front of the walls of Rome. While there he learned to his dismay

> ... that the very land on which he had encamped had just been sold at no loss of value whatsoever. It seemed to him to be such supercilious insolence for a buyer to have been found for the very land which he himself occupied... (Livy, bk. 26, chap. 11, trans. Hadas and Poe).

Though our foes see us as dying, we Catholics know that the first Resurrection presaged many another in his Mystical Body, the Church. And in one of these future resurrections of the Mystical Body, the beginnings of which it may please God that we ourselves shall see, perhaps Christian civilization will again have another day of glory.

This book is not a complete treatise on the state or the relations between Church and state. It deals with only a limited aspect of the subject. Of works known to me, the closest to this book is E. Cahill, S. J.'s *The Framework of a Christian State* (Dublin: Gill, 1932). Fr. Cahill's work, however, is more of an historical account than this present effort of mine, and on the whole more general in its discussion of the character of a Christian state.

Lastly, I wish to thank those individuals who in any way helped this book move from vision to reality, especially all those who read parts of the manuscript and aided me with suggestions, in particular, Rupert Ederer, Kirk Kramer, and my wife, Inez Storck, who in addition, before the English version was available, translated portions of the *Catechism of the Catholic Church* for me from the French.

Thomas Storck
Feast of the Most Holy Trinity, 1998

I

State and Culture

A full Christian life is one lived out in one's art,
one's politics, the form one's city takes, and any
check placed on public expression of one's Christianity is an attack on the possibility of living an
integrated life, an attempt to disallow Christian
maturation.   — *Glen W. Olsen*[1]

T HE SUBJECT OF THIS BOOK IS A
Catholic political order or a Catholic state, that
is, a regime which explicitly accepts the Catholic
faith as true, acknowledges its duty to honor Almighty God,
and seeks via its laws to protect and foster the practice of
that faith. The rationale for such a state has two parts, one
rooted in the nature of the state itself, the other in the state's
necessary role as protector of a society or culture. The first
of these, the state's immediate duties toward God, are well
stated in Leo XIII's 1885 encyclical, *Immortale Dei*.

> [T]he State, constituted as it is, is clearly bound
> to act up to the manifold and weighty duties link-
> ing it to God, by the public profession of religion.
> Nature and reason, which command every individ-
> ual devoutly to worship God in holiness, because
> we belong to Him and must return to Him, since
> from Him we came, bind also the civil community

---

[1] "The Meaning of Christian Culture, a Historical View" in David
Schindler, ed., *Catholicism and Secularization in America* (Huntington,
Indiana: Our Sunday Visitor, 1990), p. 108.

by a like law. For, men, living together in society are under the power of God no less than individuals are, and society, no less than individuals, owes gratitude to God who gave it being and maintains it and whose ever-bounteous goodness enriches it with countless blessings. Since, then, no one is allowed to be remiss in the service due to God, and since the chief duty of all men is to cling to religion in both its teaching and practice — not such religion as they may have a preference for, but the religion which God enjoins, and which certain and most clear marks show to be the only one true religion — it is a public crime to act as though there were no God . . . or out of many forms of religion to adopt that one which chimes in with the fancy; for we are bound absolutely to worship God in that way which He has shown to be His will. (no. 6)

Although the state is an association involving multiple persons, neither the persons themselves, nor the corporate body that they constitute, is somehow freed from our obligations toward our Creator. If a single person has duties toward God, there is no reason to suppose that two persons or any number of persons do not have such duties, and not simply as so many individuals, but as parts of whatever corporate body they belong to — since "men, living together in society are under the power of God no less than individuals are."

But the state or *polis* is not merely any association of individuals, it is unique and has a unique role to play in human social affairs. As a result, the state's fulfillment or lack of fulfillment of its duties to God has very important consequences for human happiness in this life and the next. Josef Pieper explains this special role of the state in the life of mankind.

The state, we may note, occupies a unique place in the scale that extends from the individual to the whole of mankind; more than anything else, it represents the "social whole." The idea of the common good is its distinctive attribute. A nation (in the midst of other nations) ordered in a state is the proper, historically concrete image of man's communal life. *Communitas politica est communitas principalissima* — Political community is community in the highest degree. In the fullest sense the state alone incorporates, realizes, and administers the *bonum commune*. That does not mean, however, that the family, the community, free associations, and the Church are not important for the realization of the common good, too. But it means that the harmonizing and integration of nearly all men's functions occurs only in the political community.[2]

Aristotle had expressed this understanding of the harmonizing task of the political community centuries earlier, when he wrote that politics, that is, the science and art of governing the *polis*,

> ordains which of the sciences should be studied in a state, and which each class of citizens should learn and up to what point they should learn them; and we see even the most highly esteemed of capacities to fall under this, e.g., strategy, economics, rhetoric. . . .[3]

This important and irreplaceable role of the *polis* is based on human nature, for to live in a political community is the natural state of mankind. Aristotle's account of the origin of

---

2   *The Four Cardinal Virtues*, (Notre Dame: University of Notre Dame, 1966), p. 85.
3   Aristotle, *Ethics*, I, 2 (Oxford translation).

society begins with the family, "established by nature for the supply of men's everyday wants," but which, "when several families are united, and the association aims at something more than the supply of daily needs," results in the village. But the village does not suffice to satisfy our requirements for a fully human life.

> When several villages are united in a single complete community, large enough to be nearly or quite self-sufficing, the state comes into existence, originating in the bare needs of life, and continuing in existence for the sake of a good life. And therefore, if the earlier forms of society are natural, so is the state, for it is the end of them, and the nature of a thing is its end.[4]

Or as Pope Leo again put it in the same encyclical, *Immortale Dei*, "Man's natural instinct moves him to live in civil society, for he cannot, if dwelling apart, provide himself with the necessary requirements of life, nor procure the means of developing his mental and moral faculties" (no. 3). But man's "mental and moral faculties" can develop in many and varied ways. The various cultures of the human race are a witness to the multiple ways that the potentialities of our nature can express themselves. Unlike the lower animals, whose behaviors are pretty much determined by their natures and the limits imposed by their environments, human nature leaves much of our conduct undetermined, so that two groups of human beings living in similar environments can express their common human nature in very different ways as a result of their diverse cultures. For example, Spanish architecture of the American Southwest attempted to build in harmony with the arid and semi-arid climate, while Anglo-Americans

---

4   *Politics*, I, 2 (Oxford translation).

often imported styles of building and expectations for living that may have worked well in New England or parts of the Midwest, but which were ill-adapted to the Southwest.

Cultural differences, however, are ultimately grounded in a culture's fundamental beliefs, in its religion or some substitute for that. As Christopher Dawson wrote, "In the last resort every civilization is built on a religious foundation: it is the expression in social institutions and cultural activity of a faith or a vision of reality which gives the civilization its spiritual unity."[5] Or as St. John Paul II expressed it in a striking passage in his encyclical *Centesimus Annus,*

> At the heart of every culture lies the attitude a person takes to the greatest mystery: the mystery of God. Different cultures are basically different ways of facing the question of the meaning of personal existence. (no. 24)

Since "the harmonizing and integration of nearly all men's functions occurs only in the political community," such a community via its organs of government becomes of the utmost importance, and the political arrangements of society shape both our cultures and our very selves. Thus one of the most important things forming the outlook of Catholics in the United States has been the American government, with its pseudo-messianic notions of a universal mission on behalf of democracy and freedom, as well as its studied indifference to Christ the King and to religion and morality in general.[6] Since by and large this messianic mythology has been accepted by Catholics as much as non-Catholics in the United States, it has been one of the

5 Christopher Dawson, *Understanding Europe* (Garden City, N.Y.: Image, 1960), p. 211.
6 I explore some of these themes in several chapters of my book, *Christendom and the West*, (Four Faces Press, 2000).

most important factors deforming the Catholic mind in America. With such ideas of government and politics reigning, how could a Catholic culture in the U. S. exist without significant defects? For unless our thinking is sound, our culture cannot be sound. With a non-Catholic government and political system, our Catholic subcultures were necessarily confused about very important matters, the relationship between the state itself and society or culture and the proper arrangements that should be made for securing the temporal common good. It is no wonder that Catholics in America have so often been resistant to Catholic social teaching, since our very political system makes it hard for them to rise above individualism and materialism. It is worthwhile, then, to look more closely at the question of why a Catholic culture is necessary and how a Catholic political order serves and protects such a culture.

The normal practice of the Catholic faith encourages or even requires community among its adherents, and will transform its external environment to reflect that community and its Faith; in other words, it will create a culture. Catholicism is not an individualistic or private religion, and though obviously a Catholic could live in a state of grace alone in an alien society or even on a desert island, this would be a very abnormal Catholic life. The Catholic Church is the Mystical Body of Jesus Christ and St. Paul describes how the different parts of the Mystical Body need each other and work together for the common good (I Cor. 12:4–31). Thus the individual and personal expression of the Faith is incomplete without the corporate, and in fact easily blends with it, as in the liturgy, which is its most perfect expression. At a minimum, Catholics have always met together for the Sacrifice of the Mass and it is difficult to imagine a situation where a group of Catholics would not go well beyond that minimum. However, in order to see what Catholics will do when they are able to express the Faith in a normal and unfettered manner, one should observe those countries and regions in which Catholicism has traditionally been the common and established religion.

In these places the numerous social and cultural activities that are natural to man as a social being are intimately bound up with the Faith, and thus there are numerous public and common celebrations and activities, institutions and organizations, in which the Faith is publicly expressed and works are carried on to further some object, spiritual or temporal, connected with the Faith. In addition to sacramental and other rituals, either in or outside the church building itself, there are numerous sodalities and confraternities, processions, pilgrimages, observances of feast days with popular devotions and other traditions such as dramas, dances, games or sports, not to mention activities to relieve or otherwise aid the poor, including charitable establishments of many kinds, cooperatives and funds for particular needs, such as dowries for poor girls. Catholicism has also hallowed many of the everyday pursuits of mankind, with blessings of houses, land, fishing fleets, tools, food and drink and numerous other items and tasks. Thus, historically, when a society has been made up of individual Catholics, it has been natural for them to express their faith not merely as so many individuals, but corporately and institutionally, by establishing institutions and forms, or changing those already existing, to reflect the Catholic religion.[7]

---

7   Compare also John Paul II's words, "A faith that does not become culture would be a faith not fully received, not entirely thought out, and not faithfully lived." Quoted in Luigi Giussani, "Religious Awareness in Modern Man," *Communio, International Catholic Review*, vol. 25, no. 1, spring 1998, p. 138. In addition, see the *Catechism of the Catholic Church*, nos. 1674–1676.

Cardinal Newman, in his book, *Certain Difficulties Felt by Anglicans in Catholic Teaching*, recounts in a striking passage such Catholic life as was lived even in 19th-century Italy.

> Once more, listen to the stories, songs, and ballads of the populace; their rude and boisterous merriment still runs upon the great invisible subjects which possess their imagination. Their ideas, of whatever sort, good, bad, and indifferent, rise out of the next world. Hence, if they would have plays, the subjects are sacred; if they would have games and sports, these fall, as it were, into procession and are formed upon the model of sacred rites and sacred persons. If they sing and jest, the Madonna and the Bambino, or St. Joseph, or St. Peter, or some other saint, is introduced, not for irreverence, but because these are the ideas that absorb them. . . . And hence, I say, in their fairs and places of amusement, in the booths, upon the stalls, upon the doors of wine-shops, will be paintings of the Blessed Virgin, or St. Michael, or the souls in purgatory, or of some Scripture subject. (vol. I, lecture 9)

No one in these traditional Catholic lands, moreover, ever supposed that a distinction could be made between the private adherence of the individual and his family to Catholicism and the public life of the country, on the grounds that religious belief was a personal matter and that, although all or nearly all citizens were Catholics, somehow their religion must be kept separate from their public life. No, for it seemed obvious to them, as indeed it should, that if the Catholic religion is really true, then it should be observed not merely by individuals and families but by all groups of men, including man organized on a cultural or political basis. It is hard to conceive how anyone who really believed

8

that the Faith was true could think that it was an ideal for society to publicly and officially ignore the Faith. How could it possibly be a benefit for organized society to ignore the most fundamental and important truths of all? Unless one has been thoroughly schooled in a false point of view, such as the American tradition of separation of dogmatic religion and government, it is doubtful whether it would ever occur to any Catholic to separate his private practice from the corporate practice of his religion.

If it is true that Catholicism in its normal state will flourish in a thousand practices and will thoroughly hallow a culture, and that this is the natural effect of the living Faith, then it follows that the natural state of a Catholic is to live in a Catholic culture, the only place where Catholic life can be lived as it ought to be lived. I do not say that many Catholics today are fortunate enough to enjoy such a situation, or even that all Catholics in the past lived in such circumstances — only that it is the milieu in which what is normal for a Catholic may be freely expressed. Obviously in non-Catholic societies a Catholic must, and usually can, adjust to the necessity of an unnatural separation between the private and the public spheres, but where Catholics are in a majority, especially an overwhelming and traditional majority, it would be very odd for fervent Catholics to establish or maintain customs or institutions that were not specifically Catholic. For example, in North America we have many civic and cultural holidays which Catholics usually observe in conjunction with the rest of the population, such as Mother's Day, Memorial Day, Labor Day, Thanksgiving and others. This seems quite natural to us. In fact we do not realize how unusual this is, how odd in historical perspective to have holidays unconnected with what we profess to be the most important thing in our lives, namely the true religion.[8] There is nothing necessarily wrong in the intent of any of the celebrations mentioned, but there is something wrong with their lack of connection with our Faith. Mother's Day, for example, could easily be on a feast day of Our Lady; Labor Day (as in Europe) on the feast of St. Joseph the Worker; Thanksgiving (as formerly in Catholic Europe) on a saint's day, and so forth. Why should we have a Catholic standard for ruling our personal or family life and a secular one for our public or civic life? The reason for this state of affairs in the United States, English-speaking Canada and elsewhere, is obviously that these are Protestant and secular lands, but where Catholics are dominant they would not act thus, unless they were misled by false theories about the proper relation between religion and cultural and political life.

So when a Catholic lives in a non-Catholic culture, whether in a secularized or other non-Catholic society, he is forced, however slightly, to restrain his expression of the Faith. How can a holy day be really observed in a non-Catholic culture, for example? Though an individual Catholic can go to Mass and perhaps even stay home from work, he knows that others are working and ignoring the holy day, that life all around him is denying what should be a public event. He cannot celebrate the holy day except as a private individual and within his family. Contrast this with an observance that is public and corporate, e.g. (in the United States) of the 4th of July or of our cultural and

---

8 See Amintore Fanfani, *Catholicism, Protestantism and Capitalism* (New York: Sheed & Ward, 1939) p. 96, for some comments on secular holidays. In most cultures holidays have always been religious — at least until modern times. Even today most European and Latin American countries have quite a few Christian holy days as official holidays. Lists of the official holidays for countries may be found in the annual two volume set, *Europa World Year Book* (London: Europa Publications).

secular celebration of Christmas. The very mood and faces of people change as Christmas approaches and the public media give their full attention to the coming holiday. Its observance is a shared cultural event. In fact, certain difficulties arise for a Catholic who is trying to observe Advent and Christmas according to the spirit of the liturgical year, for it is simply assumed that everyone will join in the secular Christmas festivities during Advent and that the celebration of Christmas ceases on December 26 or so. But the point here is that it *is* proper for holidays to be corporate celebrations. It is not fitting that the Catholic observance of the Assumption or the Immaculate Conception must be merely private events, unrecognized by either the culture or the state.[9] For of course the Protestant and secular regimes and cultures naturally recognize their holidays and ignore ours. But this troubles, or should trouble, a Catholic, for how can his religion, a religion that demands public and corporate expression to be itself, exist in a healthy manner when that public expression is prohibited or at least hampered? What non-Catholic culture will carefully observe the Church's liturgical calendar in its holidays and seasons; for example, in its decorations and displays, in the closing of shops and schools and the cessation of public business? Any non-Catholic culture will instead honor its own heroes and celebrate its own triumphs, either political and nationalistic as among us, or, as in pagan Rome or even today in India, those of alien religions.

---

9 In Europe Catholic holy days first became official state holidays in the reign of the Emperor Theodosius (379–395). "The feast days of the Church became public holidays and Lent a holy season." Philip Hughes, *A Popular History of the Catholic Church* (New York: Macmillan, c. 1947) p. 37. The *Catechism of the Catholic Church* states (no. 2188), " . . . Christians should seek recognition of Sundays and the Church's holy days as legal holidays."

Moreover, it is in more than simply public celebrations that Catholicism makes its influence felt in a culture. For, as I noted above, a culture is nothing less than the entire way of life of a people, including their legal and educational systems, their economics, their attitude toward technology, how they plan their cities and build their houses, and of course, their art and music and literature. And since the most basic constituent of a culture, the one that shapes it throughout, is its theological orientation, its religion or its secular substitute for religion, it follows that Catholicism, when it is free to be itself, will shape a culture's educational and economic systems as surely as it will determine which public holidays will be observed. It was no accident, for example, that capitalism and the industrial revolution arose in the newly Protestant lands, while in Catholic Europe the culture, often without even knowing why, clung to a way of life more in harmony with the nature of man as well as with the natural world in which we live.[10]

This then is the first and most important reason for a Catholic culture, to allow the full and free expression and

---

10   In the period during which capitalism was becoming well established in Europe, many recognized its basic incompatibility with the Catholic faith. An English writer in 1671 stated, "There is a kind of natural unaptness in the Popish religion to business...," while another Englishman, Lawrence Braddon, wrote in 1717, "The superstition of their religion obligeth France to keep (at least) fifty Holy days more than we are obliged to keep; and every such day wherein no work is done is one hundred and twenty thousand pounds loss to the deluded people." Both of these are quoted in Richard Tawney, *Religion and the Rise of Capitalism* (New York, Harcourt, Brace, 1926), pp. 206 and 315. Granted that these are hostile witnesses, but they seem to be stating what was considered a commonplace.

Less recognized is the connection between Catholicism and an attitude toward the natural world (the world of created natures) which is more benign than the Cartesian exploitation that has been the norm in the West for the past two hundred and more years. See Thomas Storck, ed. *The Glory of the Cosmos: A Catholic Approach to the Natural World,* (Arouca Press, 2020).

flowering of Catholicism: in public celebrations, in its influence on a thousand things, from education to politics, from economic activity to marriage. And in this influence on both the big and little things of life, one can see the second reason for a Catholic culture, the protection of the individual believer from error and sin.

This second reason for a Catholic culture, though obviously closely related to the first one, is what might be called its protective and negative one, namely, to prevent error and evil in the life of the individual Catholic. Thus a Catholic culture is of great importance for the individual, since it reinforces him in the Faith, reminds him of doctrinal truths necessary for living a holy life, and helps him to remember to dedicate his whole being and life and work to God. Moreover, it continually declares, by its customs, laws and institutions, even by its very material objects, that religion is not something to be put into a small box or allowed into only one compartment of life. Whether it be the blessing of tools, the existence of a roadside shrine or a public procession, all these public manifestations of the Faith remind us of the fact that God exists, that his Church teaches us truths necessary to gain Heaven and avoid Hell, and that only through our daily living of the Gospel can we hope to save our souls.

Moreover, more than we like to admit, our surrounding culture influences and conditions how we think. It frames questions for us, structures debates and sets limits to what we consider acceptable answers and solutions. For example, on the subject of regulation of the economy, our present culture in the United States puts the question to us as follows: How much should the government regulate the economy or how much should the economy be left merely to the free play of competition? As a result of the way the question is raised, our answers generally address only the amount of government activity, whether they favor little or much government regulation. The question as put by the culture does not even consider the possibility of substantive regulation by anyone but the government, for example, by the intermediary groups which papal teaching has called for. So most of us are engaged in a sterile debate on a question which, as far as Catholic thought is concerned, was never even properly framed. But most people are not prepared to look beyond the terms in which a question is put to them.

What we might call a culture's reigning ideas, that is, its most basic theological and philosophical orientations, and what can be deduced from them, pretty much determine the shape of a culture's institutions, including the political structure, the legal system, the economic system, the schools, even the role of art and music and of science and technology. No one can deny that the materialistic, naturalistic society of the United States, with its emphasis on what is considered efficient and up-to-date, influenced the thinking of Catholics in America well before the Second Vatican Council on questions such as the separation of Church and state, the place of commercialism in public and personal life, and the aims and forms of education.[11] This is largely the influence

---

11 In 1937 Robert M. Hutchins, President of the University of Chicago, gave an address to the National Catholic Educational Association Midwest Regional Meeting on "The Integrating Principle of Catholic Higher Education." He charged that Catholic education in the United States had "imitated the worst features of secular education," namely "athleticism and collegiatism." The former, of course, is football and other sports, the latter is "the production of well-tubbed young Americans. They don't have much in their heads, but are acceptable as decorations of at least one political party and make good additions to a house-party." He went on to say, "What I say is that Catholic education is not Catholic enough. The Catholic Church has the longest intellectual tradition of any institution in the contemporary world, the only uninterrupted tradition and the

of Protestantism. Today, however, secularism is doing the same thing, especially in matters such as abortion, divorce and homosexual activity, — and lately even the grotesque practice of bodily mutilation for those who feel they somehow possess bodies of the wrong sex — to condition the thinking even of believing Catholics, and this in countries formerly Catholic as well as those formerly Protestant.

Secularism allows the individual and indeed entire civilizations, to live without reference to God or to anything supernatural. A secularized person in a secularized society either finds it very difficult even to discuss the question of whether God might exist, or if he does recognize the fact that there is a God, he is practically unable to look upon religion as anything but a minor compartment in his life. It never occurs to him that his relations with God are the most important matters there are. Each area of his life he thinks about separately, and, for example, in his business greed and power are his main motives; in personal matters, pleasure; and in his vague attentions to religion, a certain emotional satisfaction is his goal. Practically he is an atheist, and though he might respond on a questionnaire that he believes in God, actually this means little or nothing to him.

Thus it is the case that a secularized society makes it hard for many or even most people not to be secularists, either explicit or practical atheists. And while we are right to aim to convert individuals to Catholicism, even in the midst of secularism, the only stable condition for the Christian believer is in a Catholic society. We have today many cases of

---

only explicit tradition. . . . What I say is that this tradition must not be merely an ideal, but must be practiced." His entire address was printed in *College Newsletter* (May 1937) and excerpts can be found in Frank L. Christ, ed., *American Catholicism and the Intellectual Ideal* (New York: Appleton-Century-Crofts, c. 1961), pp. 109–111.

persons Catholic in faith but non-Catholic in culture, and non-Catholic to a degree that almost all practical expressions of their religion, beyond the purely personal, are made null and void by their non-Catholic culture. Even persons who accept all that the Church dogmatically teaches and seek to avoid sin on a purely individual level, in every area beyond the personal too often think and act as non-Catholics. For example, they see the purpose of education as increased income for the individual or productivity for their nation. All learning for them must be justified by its immediate practical fruits. The notion of speculative knowledge as knowledge meant simply for contemplation, or even of learning as a perfection of one's intellect, is entirely foreign to them. Why? Because the utilitarian culture they live in frames all discussions about education within certain boundaries, which take for granted that all learning must be for some fairly immediate practical purpose. And unless a man has a particularly vigorous mind he will rarely be able to attend to first principles enough to think beyond the bounds in which his society has posed a question.

And if this is the situation of those who still accept what the Church teaches, what of other Catholics? As public opinion polls show, very few of them can be counted on to hold any central point, either of dogma or of morals. Whether it is the ordination of women, abortion or especially the use of contraceptives, their opinions are not very different from those of their fellow countrymen. And while the lack of firm dogmatic preaching within the Church is doubtless in part responsible, I think that their life within purely secular surroundings bears much responsibility for their sad condition.

A culture can subtly impose its limits on us in many other ways. In religion it can make us tend to think that the purpose and justification for a religion is how well it makes us behave; that religion is merely an elaborate mechanism to promote morality, or even to produce peace of mind. This notion, of course, leads to a kind of indifferentism that is interested in results, not truth. In political matters, a culture of liberalism seems to be able easily to convince most people that the notion that government or the laws might have some concern with morality or even with religion, or some explicit duty toward Almighty God, is too bizarre to be worth refuting.[12]

Catholics need to do more than simply accept the dogmatic and moral teachings of the Church if they are to avoid the situations I have just described. Although intensive

---

12 I must make it clear that by liberalism I mean the political and social philosophy and outlook that arose during the Protestant revolt of the 16th century and received its mature expression in the so-called Enlightenment of the late 17th and the 18th centuries. This political and social force includes both what we in the United States call liberalism and what we call conservativism. "In America both liberals and conservatives appealed to the same liberal founding and documents. Thus, conservatism in the United States has upheld the basic tenets of classic Anglo-Saxon and continental liberalism regarding the absolute rights of individuals, the privatization of religion, and a supposed impossibility of resolving the question of truth in serious disputes regarding morality and religion." Matthew Lamb, "Modernism and Americanism Revisited Dialectically: A Challenge for Evangelization," *Communio, International Catholic Review*, vol. 21, no. 4, winter 1994, pp. 647–648.

Liberalism began as a revolt against Christian economic morality and by now is attacking the family and chastity. It really has no doctrines per se, except to break down Christian civilization, and it is necessarily secularistic, i.e. a-religious. Nearly the whole of the modern world is built upon this liberalism, and it is today the chief enemy of the Church within Western culture. Whenever I speak of "liberals" or "liberalism" in this work, I am using the words in this sense. See Louis Cardinal Billot, *Liberalism, A Critique of Its Basic Principles and Various Forms* (Arouca Press, 2019), and my book, *From Christendom to Americanism and Beyond* (Angelico Press, 2017).

catechizing and other educational efforts are important for forming the faithful to be Catholic in every area of their lives, the best, the normal, and, for the vast majority of men, the only secure way to accomplish this, is to create a Catholic culture. Only in a Catholic civilization will the unconscious lessons that all cultures teach not just reinforce the Faith, but also mold our thinking into Catholic patterns. It is of course necessary for Catholics to accept the dogmatic and moral teachings of the hierarchical Magisterium, but this is not enough, nor is it enough to "accept Catholic social teaching," for example. What must be done is for Catholics to be initiated into a way of thought and life, that is, into a culture, into Catholic culture. Of course, if a living Catholic culture actually existed anywhere in the world today, then those Catholics residing there could easily achieve such initiation and attain an integrated Catholic outlook. But for most of us, in secularized cultures or disintegrating Catholic cultures, we must make conscious efforts to form our own souls in a Catholic manner, to organize our thoughts, our lives, and as much as possible and on as wide a scale as possible, our surroundings, so that they are thoroughly Catholic. Only in this way can we begin to create a normal atmosphere for a Catholic life, an atmosphere that will nourish and strengthen our faith.

The reason that this aspect of a Catholic culture is necessary, what I call its protective and negative function, is the fact of original sin and its consequences. Because of original sin our intellects are darkened and their control over our appetites weak, our personal sins have further weakened our natures, and the long heritage of human error and sin simply reinforces these individual weaknesses, so that all of us are susceptible to error and occasions of sin. And it is precisely the removal of some of these occasions of sin which a Catholic culture, protected by a Catholic state, can hope to accomplish. Quite obviously such a regime and civilization cannot remove all occasions of sin. But wise law, supported by and supporting a Catholic culture, can do much. Though a Catholic political order without real faith on the part of its members is ultimately empty and futile, if it is protecting a living Catholic culture it is of immense value, for the cultural by itself is vulnerable without the political.

Granted, then, the desirability of a Catholic culture, it is not difficult to see why a Catholic state is necessary to safeguard it. Man must live under some political arrangement, indeed he cannot perfect himself without the political, and unless that arrangement is Catholic, it will be non-Catholic and ultimately anti-Catholic. A Catholic culture cannot safely exist under non-Catholic rulers, for even if it is tolerated for a time, there is no security for such a culture. The rulers may seek to destroy it at any time they choose or, more likely, to harass and restrict it so that ultimately it is reduced to a nullity.[13]

But even were non-Catholic political authorities not actively hostile in their attitude toward a Catholic culture, would they really permit the proper celebration of a Holy Day, for example? Would they permit business to be

---

13 "The community is the dimension and condition necessary for the human seed to bear fruit. For this reason, we can say that the true, the most intelligent persecution, is not the one employed by Nero and his amphitheatre of wild beasts or the concentration camp. The most ferocious persecution is the modern state's attempt to block the expression of the communital dimension of the religious phenomenon. As far as the state is concerned, a person can, in conscience, believe what he likes, as long as this faith does not imply that all believers are one, and therefore, have the right to live and express this reality. To obstruct communital expression is like cutting off the roots that nourish the plant: the plant soon dies." Luigi Giussani, *The Religious Sense* (Montreal: McGill-Queen's University, 1997), p. 131.

disrupted, streets clogged for processions, municipal services perhaps interrupted? I do not say they would always positively prohibit such things; but without official recognition, the simple pressures of life would make it very difficult for all but the most militant Catholics to stay away from work and take part in such a celebration.[14] For here, as in other matters, it is the subtle interaction and mutual support of culture and law that gives stability to a way of life in a nation. It has more than once been said that laws are useless without the support of custom, and surely this is true. But custom also needs the framework of law to support it, because if the law ignores it or tries to crush it, then custom can rarely stand up to it for long. For even if Catholicism itself is able to withstand the force of law, as it did in Ireland under English oppression or in Poland under Communist rule, the evil laws will deprive the Faith of that cultural expression which is crucial to forming Catholics and a Catholic society. In short, although the Faith may survive under an anti-Catholic regime, an integral Catholic culture cannot.[15]

---

14   Fr. Edward Cahill, in his monumental work, *The Framework of a Christian State* observed with regard to the question of holy days as public holidays that "a Christian Government will safeguard the observance of the Lord's Day and the holydays of the Church, by removing from the people's way the need, or temptation, to violate them" (p. 607). It is right that since man is weak and thus prone to sin, human law and custom should protect him and help him toward his final end.

15   The difficulty which Poland had in outlawing abortion several years after the overthrow of Communism is a good example of how non-Catholic political arrangements poison the national life and accustom people to the easy acceptance of evils.

The island of Guam, a U. S. possession, is about 90% Catholic. Yet with the exception of January 1 and Christmas Day, all of its holidays are secular, being mainly the same as official U. S. holidays. In contrast, in secularized Sweden, the following are among the official holidays: January 1, Epiphany, Good Friday, Easter Monday, Ascension Day,

The point is that a non-Catholic political framework never can and never will understand the Catholic point of view and the necessity for the full expression of Catholic faith. The difficulty of allowing Catholics to fully observe the liturgical year by the proper celebration of holy days has been mentioned. In another area, the non-Catholic political order will always be tending to make just one or two seemingly very sensible exceptions on such matters as divorce or abortion. It is very hard for most non-Catholics to grasp that Christ's law against divorce or abortion allows no exceptions whatsoever, for to their way of thinking it is insanity to prohibit divorce when a wife (say) has escaped from a drunken husband and wants to begin her life over again, or to disallow abortion for a victim of rape. Yet a Catholic way of life obviously will follow the law of God on both these matters, and it is right that such a way of life be protected by human laws framed according to the truth.

In the remainder of this book, then, I will take up what this role of protecting and perfecting a Catholic culture might

---

the Monday after Pentecost, All Saints, Christmas Day, Feast of St. Stephen! Obviously this is simply a holdover from Sweden's Catholic days, but to the extent that it gives the opportunity for corporate recognition of certain sacred days and events, it is a good. The U. S., with its secularized culture *ab initio*, never developed such Catholic cultural practices, and because of its political connection with Guam, that unfortunate island is made to share our secular heritage. And even though Guam is predominantly Catholic, her Catholic life is vitiated to the extent that its political connections impede corporate observance of holy days. More seriously, because of her association with the United States, Guam sustains numerous other direct evil influences from the mainland. For example, the Guam Federation of Teachers is associated with the anti-Catholic American Federation of Teachers.

And it is not merely Guam into which the secular political regime of the United States has intruded its evils. The U. S. introduced divorce and legal abortion into Catholic Puerto Rico as well.

actually look like. What would be the powers and duties of a Catholic state, what special institutions might it create or foster, what would be the spirit of its approach to governing? Necessarily much that will be discussed in subsequent chapters will concern restrictions and limits on men's behavior. No state is without its laws and police, so this will come as no surprise. But I should emphasize that these restraints should be seen as the framework, made necessary largely by original sin,[16] within which Catholicism should be able to flower in freedom. A Catholic state, as I said, exists to make possible a Catholic culture. So while much of the work of the state *is* negative, the work of the culture, although it has its restraining aspects, is for the most part positive, in that it is an expression of Catholic life. But we should keep in mind that both a Catholic political order and a Catholic culture will facilitate the flowering of Catholic life on the part of both individuals and groups.

I think, however, that it is necessary to discuss briefly how we should regard these legal restrictions on our conduct, for when this question of restrictions on freedom of behavior is mentioned in the West today, this is seen as a challenge to the central dogma of contemporary culture and of the liberal state, a dogma well-expressed by Fr. Robert Sirico of the Acton Institute that, "So long as individuals avoid forceful or fraudulent actions in their dealings with one another, government is to stay out of their business,"[17] or by another writer, that "each of us should be able to do pretty much what

---

16 I do not mean to imply that had the Fall never occurred there would now be *no* government at all, simply that such a government would not need to restrict men's behavior so much as to coordinate it. See St. Thomas, *Summa Theologiae* I, q. 96, art. 4, and what I said above about the positive role of the political power.

17 *Acton Notes*, vol. 8, no. 1, January 1998, p. 1.

she or he wants."[18] And this dogma is more entrenched in most of our minds than perhaps we like to think. The notion that the state and its laws exist to point us toward virtue and help us attain it is entirely foreign to our way of thinking. This, of course, is in large part because we do not think man has any virtue, that is, any intrinsic purpose or perfection of which his separate virtues are aspects or manifestations. We also no longer know the reason why people live together in community, so it is no surprise that we do not know the purpose of a community or of its laws. The extent to which modern notions of man and the state are departures from Christian and classical teaching is astounding. Only when we get rid of the idea that "each of us should be able to do pretty much what she or he wants," *not* because one wants to impose a totalitarian regime, but because even our legitimate and necessary freedoms must be looked at in a different light, can we begin to understand the truth of this matter.

We are apt to regard *freedom to err* as of the essence of freedom, forgetting that the ability to do so is not necessary to our freedom nor an essential sign of it, for, as Leo XIII pointed out, " . . . the pursuit of what has a false appearance of good, though a proof of our freedom, just as a disease is a proof of our vitality, implies defect in human liberty."[19] Our Lord had perfect freedom of will, yet could not sin. The purpose of our freedom is to allow us to choose the good.

In addition, too often the freedom of choice that necessarily accompanies any rational creature has been seen as in conflict, at least potentially, with the needs of the community. For example, it is plausible, but incorrect, to say that our freedom is limited by the legitimate requirements of

---

18   Mary Doyle, in "From Russia, With Doubts" *Legal Times*, November 26, 1990, p. 24.
19   Encyclical *Libertas Praestantissimum*, no. 6.

living together in a community, as if the community and our proper freedom could be in conflict. It is even worse to say that by a kind of bargain or contract we limit our natural freedom to gain the advantages of living in society. It is not our freedom, but a distortion of our freedom, that demands a right to act contrary to the good. In fact, when a political community restrains man's activities, we should not think of this as a restriction on our freedom but as a guiding of it toward both the common good as well as our own good. A choice of evil is not an exercise of our rational freedom but an abuse of it.

At least in Anglo-Saxon countries, Catholics, even orthodox ones, are for the most part infected with the surrounding political liberalism, that is, with political ideas that descend through John Locke, and which involve the notion of the social contract and of the bargain, at least theoretical and implicit, made by each individual to give up some of his natural freedom and thereby obtain the benefits of society. With this point of view every restriction of our desires and appetites is seen as a restriction of that natural freedom, even if we consider the restriction justified in this or that case. Those who hold the liberal or Lockean viewpoint are disposed to regard suspiciously every law limiting what they suppose is their natural freedom. The burden of proof is always on those making the law, and as a result we have today in the West totally irresponsible conduct in our societies; for example, in the economy, we have conduct which aims merely to enrich the individual, but does nothing to fulfill the intrinsic purpose of economic activity, supplying needed goods and services, and that frequently even injures the common good; and, equally, in publishing or otherwise disseminating opinions and in entertainment and the arts, we have material which causes harm to the community, however much it may gratify its producers and enrich its distributors. This distorted notion of freedom has even influenced our daily social interactions, as we see an increasing unwillingness to accept any restrictions on the fulfillment of our desires, and less and less does anyone seem to want to restrain himself for the sake of the common good.

Although it would require a sea change in the attitudes of most Catholics, yet this is necessary if we wish ever to re-establish a Catholic culture protected and ordered by a Catholic state. The next few chapters, then, which deal with restrictions on our religious behavior, on our economic activity and on our expression of opinions and our artistic activity, should be looked at in this light, that they do not so much restrict as provide order or structure for our true freedom. I do not deny, of course, that governments too often impose restraints which the common good does not demand, and which are even opposed to the common good, but the existence of such unjust or petty laws should not bring us to see the state as our enemy or to look at laws with an individualistic eye. If we remember that our own nature requires that the laws direct us toward the common good, then we can look at stupid or unjust laws as so many impediments toward the harmonious functioning of the community and not primarily as impositions on our individual freedom. It is the community's good which is violated here as much as the individual's, and we can oppose such wrongs without taking refuge in Lockean individualism or liberal theories of the state.[20]

---

20 This is not to say that the police in a Catholic state will force everyone to obey every precept of the moral law. St. Thomas, for example, asks the question whether the civil law should repress all vices and answers in the negative. See *Summa Theologiae* I–II, q. 96, art. 1, 2 and 3.

2

Religious Liberty

There was once a time when States were governed
by the philosophy of the Gospel. Then it was that
the power and divine virtue of Christian wisdom
had diffused itself throughout the laws, institutions,
and morals of the people, permeating all ranks and
relations of civil society. Then, too, the religion
instituted by Jesus Christ, established firmly in befitting dignity, flourished everywhere, by the favor of
princes and the legitimate protection of magistrates;
and Church and State were happily united in concord and friendly interchange of good offices.
— Leo XIII, *Immortale Dei*, no. 21

I

THIS CHAPTER IS CERTAINLY THE
most crucial of this book, for in it will be discussed
the question of whether and how a Catholic state
may favor and support the one true religion, the Catholic
faith, and on the other hand, restrict the expression of false,
i.e., non-Catholic, religions. This question is of supreme
importance because the conception of a culture unified
around Catholic truth, and expressing that truth publicly
through a variety of customs, institutions and practices of
all sorts, would seem to be seriously compromised by at least
certain types of public expression and advocacy of religious
error. The continual public manifestation of non-Catholic
religions, even more so their promotion, would profoundly

alter the character of a Catholic society. There would be the possibility that some—or even great numbers—would be led astray from the true Faith, the very face of the society would no longer be a Catholic one, but to some degree would need to accommodate itself to error, an attitude that is not far from conceding that on some level the culture may prescind from concern about which is the true religion. In addition, the question of religious liberty is obviously important for any discussion of censorship, which is the topic of chapter four, because the degree and type of censorship will depend in part on what decisions are made on freedom of proselytizing and of public worship by non-Catholics.

The question of the recognition of Catholic truth by the culture as a whole, and particularly by the state or government, is important also because of what it implies about man's duty to God. As I pointed out in the previous chapter, Catholic teaching has always held that the political community was not exempt from the duty that obligates each one of its members as individuals to render to Almighty God that worship which he himself desires. And even apart from the teaching of the Church, it is hard to see why man organized into a political community should be able to officially ignore his Creator and Redeemer — or, for that matter, why he would even want to ignore the true source of his highest benefits. But if a body of non-Catholics is able to publicly worship, and especially to try to propagate their faith, then, as I said, what was before a society whose every institution and custom expressed and embodied Catholic truth, now, to some degree at least, those institutions and customs must make allowance for error. Any lessening of the public, corporate adherence to the true Faith disturbs and disfigures a Catholic society.

Now the Church's traditional teaching did full justice to this conception of a Catholic state and a Catholic society. In particular, several nineteenth and twentieth century popes taught explicitly the value of such an arrangement, and condemned a religious neutral society, except as that was made necessary for other reasons, such as preserving civil peace. Let us look at several key passages from some of these papal documents. The first instance is from the *Syllabus of Errors* of Pope Pius IX (1846 to 1878), December 8, 1864. The *Syllabus* is a list of condemned propositions, so in each case what is affirmed by the Pope is the contradictory of the proposition stated.

> no. 77. In the present day it is no longer expedient that the Catholic religion should be held as the only religion of the State, to the exclusion of all other forms of worship.

> no. 78. Hence it has been wisely decided by law, in some Catholic countries, that persons coming to reside therein shall enjoy the public exercise of their own peculiar worship.

> no. 79. Moreover, it is false that the civil liberty of every form of worship, and the full power, given to all, of overtly and publicly manifesting any opinions whatsoever and thoughts, conduce more easily to corrupt the morals and minds of the people, and to propagate the pest of indifferentism.

Pius IX's successor on the chair of Peter, Leo XIII (1878–1903), approached this question in a systematic way, issuing a series of encyclicals on the major political and social problems of his day, and indeed of all days. He treated the question of the duty of states and societies to offer true worship to God several times, as also the related question of the toleration of erroneous forms of worship. Appropriate quotations from these encyclicals are as follows:

As a consequence, the State, constituted as it is, is clearly bound to act up to the manifold and weighty duties linking it to God, by the public profession of religion. Nature and reason, which command every individual devoutly to worship God in holiness, because we belong to Him and must return to Him, since from Him we came, bind also the civil community by a like law. For, men, living together in society are under the power of God no less than individuals are, and society, no less than individuals, owes gratitude to God who gave it being and maintains it and whose ever-bounteous goodness enriches it with countless blessings. Since, then, no one is allowed to be remiss in the service due to God, and since the chief duty of all men is to cling to religion in both its teaching and practice — not such religion as they may have a preference for, but the religion which God enjoins, and which certain and most clear marks show to be the only one true religion — it is a public crime to act as though there were no God . . . or out of many forms of religion to adopt that one which chimes in with the fancy; for we are bound absolutely to worship God in that way which He has shown to be His will.

— Immortale Dei, no. 6

There was once a time when States were governed by the philosophy of the Gospel. Then it was that the power and divine virtue of Christian wisdom had diffused itself throughout the laws, institutions, and morals of the people, permeating all ranks and relations of civil society. Then, too, the religion instituted by Jesus Christ, established firmly in befitting dignity, flourished everywhere, by the favor of princes and the legitimate protection of magistrates; and Church and State

were happily united in concord and friendly interchange of good offices.

—*Immortale Dei*, no. 21.

. . . that it is not lawful for the State, any more than
for the individual, either to disregard all religious
duties or to hold in equal favor different kinds of
religion. . . .

—*Immortale Dei*, no. 35.

But, to justify [liberty of worship], it must needs
be taken as true that the State has no duties toward
God, or that such duties, if they exist, can be aban-
doned with impunity, both of which assertions are
manifestly false. For it cannot be doubted but that,
by the will of God, men are united in civil society;
whether its component parts be considered; or its
form, which implies authority; or the object of
its existence; or the abundance of the vast services
which it renders to man. God it is who has made
man for society, and has placed him in the company
of others like himself, so that what was wanting
to his nature, and beyond his attainment if left
to his own resources, he might obtain by association with others. Wherefore, civil society must
acknowledge God as its Founder and Parent, and
must obey and reverence His power and authority.
Justice therefore forbids, and reason itself forbids,
the State to be godless; or to adopt a line of action
which would end in godlessness—namely, to treat
the various religions (as they call them) alike, and
to bestow upon them promiscuously equal rights
and privileges. Since, then, the profession of one
religion is necessary in the State, that religion must
be professed which alone is true. . . .

—*Libertas Praestantissimum*, no. 21.

Yet, with the discernment of a true mother, the Church weighs the great burden of human weakness, and well knows the course down which the minds and actions of men are in this our age being borne. For this reason, while not conceding any right to anything save what is true and honest, she does not forbid public authority to tolerate what is at variance with truth and justice, for the sake of avoiding some greater evil, or of obtaining or preserving some greater good.... But if, in such circumstances, for the sake of the common good (and this is the only legitimate reason), human law may or even should tolerate evil, it may not and should not approve or desire evil for its own sake; for evil of itself, being a privation of good, is opposed to the common welfare which every legislator is bound to desire and defend to the best of his ability.

—*Libertas Praestantissimum*, no. 33.[1]

It remains to quote parts of an address by Pope Pius XII (1939 to 1958), *Ci Riesce*, given on December 6, 1953 to a convention of the Union of Italian Catholic Jurists.

Could God, although it would be possible and easy for Him to repress error and moral deviation, in some cases choose the *non impedire* without contradicting His infinite perfection? Could it be that *in certain circumstances* He would not give men any mandate, would not impose any duty, and

---

1   These are the chief Leonine texts, but there are other relevant passages, which I merely mention here in order not to make the text unduly long: *Humanum Genus*, nos. 22, 24, *Immortale Dei*, no. 32, *Libertas Praestantissimum*, nos. 18, 19–30, *Longinqua Oceani*, no. 6. Also several encyclicals of Pius XI (reigned 1922 to 1939) restate these truths on the duties of the state toward Christ and the true faith; they include *Ubi Arcano*, no. 22 and *Quas Primas*, nos. 8 and 20.

would not even communicate the right to impede or to repress what is erroneous and false? A look at things as they are gives an affirmative answer.

Pope Pius goes on to say,

> The duty of repressing moral and religious error cannot therefore be an ultimate norm of action. It must be subordinate to *higher and more general* norms which *in some circumstances* permit, and even perhaps seem to indicate as the better policy, toleration of error in order to promote *a greater good*.

And the next paragraph contains the following assertion:

> ... that which does not correspond to truth or to the norm of morality objectively has no right to exist, to be spread, or to be activated.

Note that there are two separate issues treated of in these statements, 1. the duty of the state to affirm the true faith and to offer worship to God, and 2. the right or duty, as the case may be, of those same political authorities to restrict in some manner the activities of non-Catholic sects and religions.[2] Although obviously connected, they are distinct, for

---

2 A good summary and defense of this pre-Vatican II teaching can be found in John A. Ryan and Francis J. Boland, *Catholic Principles of Politics* (New York: Macmillan, 1947, pp. 311–321). This is the same Fr. John Ryan who was the foremost advocate of the Church's teaching on social and economic justice in the United States. For a time during the 1920s he was a national board member of the American Civil Liberties Union and was later a member of the Industrial Appeals Board of the National Recovery Administration, an agency established as part of Franklin Roosevelt's New Deal. In our confused and misleading use of political labels in the United States, he is often called a liberal. Yet as a faithful son of the Church, he upheld the teaching of Leo XIII and the other popes. See his interesting autobiography, *Social Doctrine in Action* (New York: Harper, 1941).

it would be possible to have a state which gave due honor to Christ according to the forms of the religion he has revealed, Catholicism, and yet which allowed some, or even complete, freedom to non-Catholic religions. After all, even such secularized liberal democracies as England and the Scandinavian countries have state churches and religious rites in the coronations of their monarchs.

As to the second point, the right or duty of restricting non-Catholic religious activity, one can see that although this duty of a Catholic government was taken for granted, yet there were circumstances in which it could not be fully carried out. Leo XIII makes clear that sometimes because of the common good "human law may or even should tolerate evil," while Pius XII affirms this, pointing out that in such cases God "would not even communicate the right to impede or to repress what is erroneous and false." But these instances were held to be exceptions to the general rule of the state's "duty of repressing moral and religious error."

Now, were these statements of Leo XIII and the other popes all that one had to deal with, there would be little room for controversy on this subject. However, there is another document which we must also consider, the Declaration on Religious Liberty, *Dignitatis Humanae* (December 7, 1965) of the Second Vatican Council.

In this document the Vatican Council seems, at least at first glance, to teach much that is contrary to the papal teaching quoted above. Here are the main points of the Declaration,

> The Vatican Council declares that the human person has a right to religious freedom. Freedom of this kind means that all men should be immune from coercion on the part of individuals, social groups and every human power so that, within due

limits, nobody is forced to act against his convictions nor is anyone to be restrained from acting in accordance with his convictions in religious matters in private or in public, alone or in association with others. The Council further declares that the right to religious freedom is based on the very dignity of the human person as known through the revealed word of God and by reason itself. This right of the human person to religious freedom must be given such recognition in the constitutional order of society as will make it a civil right.

... Therefore the right to religious freedom has its foundation not in the subjective attitude of the individual but in his very nature. For this reason the right to this immunity continues to exist even in those who do not live up to their obligations of seeking the truth and adhering to it. The exercise of this right cannot be interfered with as long as the just requirements of public order are observed. no. 2.

... Consequently to deny man the free exercise of religion in society, when the just requirements of public order are observed, is to do an injustice to the human person and to the very order established by God for men.... no. 3.

The freedom or immunity from coercion in religious matters which is the right of individuals must also be accorded to men when they act in community....

Religious communities have the further right not to be prevented from publicly teaching and bearing witness to their beliefs by the spoken or written word....

> Also included in the right to religious freedom is
> the right of religious groups not to be prevented
> from freely demonstrating the special value of their
> teaching for the organization of society and the
> inspiration of all human activity. no. 4.

However, in the very first section of the Declaration occurs
this sentence:

> So while the religious freedom which men demand
> in fulfilling their obligation to worship God has to
> do with freedom from coercion in civil society, it
> leaves intact the traditional Catholic teaching on
> the moral duty of individuals and societies toward
> the true religion and the one Church of Christ.

My method in this chapter will be as follows. I will
consider this seeming contradiction between *Dignitatis
Humanae* and the earlier teaching, attempting to make
sense of the situation and arguing for what seems to me
to be the truth of this matter. Then in the second part of
the chapter I will draw out the conclusions as to how this
might shape the laws and policies of a Catholic state in the
field of religious freedom.

Since both the papal teaching here in question and the
decree of the Second Vatican Council are examples of the
teaching of the Church's Magisterium, it would seem that
any loyal Catholic should first try to see if those teachings
can be harmonized. Now, while there is much in *Dignitatis Humanae* that certainly differs in tone from the earlier
teaching, and even seems to differ in content, one must take a
close look at that document to see what is actually demanded
by its teaching.

In the first place, then, I would suggest that *Dignitatis Humanae* is not as easily understood as it seems at first

glance. Although most of the document speaks of man's right to religious freedom, yet it also contains the statement, quoted above, that "the traditional Catholic teaching on the moral duty of individuals and societies towards the true religion and the one Church of Christ" is left unchanged by this document's teaching on religious freedom. Yet this "traditional teaching" is precisely the matter of the encyclicals and other documents of Pius IX, Leo XIII, Pius XI and Pius XII. In other words, *Dignitatis Humanae* explicitly affirms the very body of teaching it is usually assumed to contradict and supplant! The greater part of *Dignitatis Humanae*, however, does not affirm traditional teaching, but speaks at length and in some detail of man's religious liberty, and in terms very different from Leo XIII. Thus, it seems to me, the task is not just to understand how the earlier papal teaching is congruent with *Dignitatis Humanae*, but how the reaffirmation of the "traditional teaching" at the beginning of *Dignitatis Humanae* is congruent with the discussion of the right to religious freedom that makes up the bulk of the document. Can these seemingly differing affirmations in the Declaration be harmonized? Does *Dignitatis Humanae* contradict itself? Let us see if the following procedure makes sense.

The affirmation of traditional teaching at the beginning of *Dignitatis Humanae* is made as a general statement that appears to be intended as an interpretative principle for the whole Declaration. If we take this affirmation seriously, then what comes after must be understood in its light. Thus we cannot attempt to understand the latter (and larger) part of *Dignitatis Humanae* absolutely and on its own, but only in the light of this statement in its first article. Now, if this is so, then certain cautions in the document can be seen in a new light.

The larger part of the Declaration on Religious Liberty (nos. 2 through 15) discusses the right to this religious freedom, but with limitations. These are the "due limits" and the "just requirements of public order," both mentioned in no. 2 (and quoted above) and an even more important statement in no. 7, which declares that religious freedom, as is the case with any other freedom exercised in society, is bound by "the rights of others" and "the common good of all." Now it may seem to some that to interpret these limitations along the lines of the teaching of Pius IX, Leo XIII and their successors might seem forced, but this is so only if one forgets what seems to me the guiding principle of interpretation of this document, the statement in the first article that "traditional Catholic teaching" is not changed. If this statement is taken at face value (and I see no reason why it should not be), then the "due limits" and the "just requirements of public order," and especially the requirement that the exercise of religious freedom is limited by "the common good of all," must mean more than they might seem to mean at first glance.

The solution, then, that I suggest is this: That the "just requirements of public order," the "due limits," and considerations of the rights of others and of the common good vary considerably from society to society, and that in a society overwhelmingly and traditionally Catholic they could easily include restrictions, and even an outright prohibition, on the public activities of non-Catholic sects, particularly on their proselytizing activities. Man's religious liberty is real and the Council's Declaration is not false or heretical; simply that the right to exercise such freedom is not the same in every place and time. A non-Catholic has the real political right, even in a Catholic state, to privately profess his own religion and privately meet with his co-religionists; in a liberal regime he has a right to considerably more freedom. In both cases the freedom is real, simply that the "requirements of public order" and especially of the common good differ.

In *Ci Riesce* Pius XII stated that the "duty of repressing moral and religious error cannot . . . be an ultimate norm of action. It must be subordinate to *higher and more general norms. . . .*" One of these more general norms is, of course, that of the common good, not only the national, but that of the Church and of the entire world. Thus obviously it could never be in accord with the common good to repress non-Catholics where they are in the majority nor even in a large or traditional minority. So while in some cases the common good would allow and might even require limitations on non-Catholic public activity, in other cases the common good permits or demands a greater degree of the exercise of liberty by non-Catholics, for, as *Dignitatis Humanae* itself states, the right to religious freedom is subject to the "common good of all" (no. 7).[3]

If this manner of interpretation seems contrived, I would simply ask how else can we make sense of the claim at the beginning of the Declaration that it is leaving "intact" the "traditional Catholic teaching" on this subject? This position that I am arguing for, moreover, receives official confirmation in the *Catechism of the Catholic Church*. Here are the relevant passages:

> Freedom is exercised in relationships between human beings. Every human person, created in the image of God, has the natural right to be recognized

---

3   Even John Courtney Murray, one of the architects of the religious liberty declaration, in commenting on this very passage, wrote, "Note that the right itself is always inalienable, never to be denied; only the exercise of the right is subject to control in particular instances." Walter Abbott, ed., *The Documents of Vatican II* (New York: Guild Press, 1966), footnote 20 on page 686.

as a free and responsible being. All owe to each other this duty of respect. The *right to the exercise of freedom*, especially in moral and religious matters, is an inalienable requirement of the dignity of the human person. This right must be recognized and protected by civil authority within the limits of the common good and public order. (no. 1738) (Emphasis in original.)

The duty of offering God genuine worship concerns man both individually and socially. This is "the traditional Catholic teaching on the moral duty of individuals and societies toward the true religion and the one Church of Christ." By constantly evangelizing men, the Church works toward enabling them "to infuse the Christian spirit into the mentality and mores, laws and structures of the communities in which [they] live." The social duty of Christians is to respect and awaken in each man the love of the true and the good. It requires them to make known the worship of the one true religion which subsists in the Catholic and apostolic Church. Christians are called to be the light of the world. Thus, the Church shows forth the kingship of Christ over all creation and in particular over human societies. (no. 2105)

The right to religious liberty can of itself be neither unlimited nor limited only by a "public order" conceived in a positivist or naturalist manner. The "due limits" which are inherent in it must be determined for each social situation by political prudence, according to the requirements of the common good, and ratified by the civil authority in accordance with "legal principles which are in conformity with the objective moral order." (no. 2109)

Paragraphs 1738 and 2109 from the *Catechism* affirm not only that the common good is the controlling principle in the regulation of religious liberty, and that "public order" may not be conceived after a merely "positivist" manner, i.e., without taking into account moral and spiritual goods, but even more to the point, that "each social situation" requires a differing estimation of the common good according to political prudence. The requirements of the common good, and thus, the type and degree of religious liberty that should be granted in "each social situation," will necessarily differ. In a culture entirely Catholic, or almost so, the requirements of the common good have traditionally been seen as demanding prohibitions, to one degree of another, on public non-Catholic religious activity, while in the different "social situation" of a non-Catholic culture, the requirements of the common good would vary accordingly. Thus *Dignitatis Humanae* can clearly be interpreted in harmony with the common teaching on religious liberty that obtained before the Second Vatican Council.[4]

I believe, then, that there is no contradiction between the teaching of the earlier popes and of *Dignitatis Humanae* rightly understood, despite the very different tone of that latter document. If we examine the Declaration carefully, as we must, and especially if we look at it in the light of the *Catechism*, then we can see that "traditional Catholic teaching on the moral duty of individuals and societies toward the true religion and the one Church of Christ" does indeed remain "intact."

---

4   The footnotes to these sections of the *Catechism* also point the way toward full acknowledgment of the continuity of the earlier teaching with that of *Dignitatis Humanae*, for they include references to *Immortale Dei* and *Libertas* of Leo XIII, *Quas Primas* of Pius XI and even *Quanta Cura* of Pius IX, the encyclical which accompanied the *Syllabus of Errors*.

II

> If there is only one true religion, and if its posses-
> sion is the most important good in life for States as
> well as individuals, then the public profession, pro-
> tection, and promotion of this religion and the legal
> prohibition of all direct assaults upon it, become
> one of the most obvious and fundamental duties
> of the State. — Msgr. John A. Ryan[5]

> We wish also to make amends . . . for the public
> crimes of nations who resist the rights and teach-
> ing authority of the Church which you have
> founded. — Prayer, *Jesu dulcissime*[6]

In this second part of the chapter, then, I will apply the
conclusions reached in the first part regarding religious liberty
in a Catholic society and state. Now in the first place, as I said
above, there are two parts to Catholic teaching on religious
liberty, as was explicit in the pre-Vatican II documents, and
which was not overruled by Vatican II. The first is the public,
official and corporate recognition by the state of the existence
of God and of the other truths of the Catholic religion, and
of the worship of God according to the religion which he

---

5   Ryan and Boland, *Catholic Principles of Politics*, p. 319.
6   This is from an indulgenced prayer listed in the post-Vatican II
compilation of indulgences, the *Enchiridion Indulgentiarum* (Vatican
City: Libreria Editrice Vaticana, 1968 and 1986). The 1969 English edition, *Enchiridion of Indulgences* (New York: Catholic Book Publishing
Co.), from which the quote here has been taken, is much more faithful
to the originals in its translations of the indulgenced prayers than the
later edition, *The Handbook of Indulgences* (New York: Catholic Book
Publishing Co., c. 1991). Although the *Handbook* is based on a later
edition of the *Enchiridion Indulgentiarum* (1986), the indulgenced
prayers are almost completely the same — saving the translations, which
were done in large part by the ICEL. The text from the prayer, *Jesu
dulcissime*, in the ICEL translation reads, "We wish to make amends . . .
for the public defiance of your law" (p. 54).

has revealed; the second is the restricting of public activities of non-Catholic religions. Now the first point, the official recognition of God and Catholic truth, in turn has two parts of its own: in the first place, the *ceremonial* recognition of God, as for example, in the opening of a session of parliament with Catholic prayers, the coronation of a monarch with Catholic rites, making holy days official state holidays, etc. In the second place is the *framing of all laws on all subjects*—economics, censorship, family law, etc.—so that they do not contradict Catholic moral teaching, and in fact so that the laws reflect and promote Catholic truth and a Catholic organization of society.[7] The bulk of this book deals with this last effort, that of framing all laws so that they aid in the preservation and perfection of a truly Catholic society.

In normal circumstances the recognition of God and of the Catholic religion should be explicit on the part of the state. For example, it should have an appropriate place in any written constitution or other fundamental law, and the nation's legal codes should contain a statement that they are to be interpreted according to Catholic moral teaching.[8]

---

7   Leo XIII, *Libertas*, no. 18. It must be remembered, though, that the state and human law are not required to attempt to ban every sin and vice of mankind. To do so in some cases would infringe too much on human freedom and in others it would be impossible to enforce, thus making the law look ridiculous. Rulers must use political prudence in framing laws. See St. Thomas, *Summa Theologiae*, I–II, q. 96, art. 2.
8   Although deficient in that it did not explicitly make Catholicism the religion of the state, nevertheless the Irish constitution of 1937 (which is still in force) contains an impressive recognition of the Holy Trinity and of our Divine Lord. It begins thus, "In the Name of the Most Holy Trinity, from Whom is all authority and to Whom, as our final end, all actions both of men and States must be referred, We, the people of Eire, humbly acknowledging all our obligations to our Divine Lord Jesus Christ. ... " Later, in Article 44, clause I (i), it states, "The State acknowledges that the homage of public worship is due to Almighty God."

By no means, though, do I think that everything that obtained in some places in the past is desirable for a Catholic state. For example, there was the practice of the nomination of bishops by the government, or at least the approval by the government of bishops chosen by the Holy See. This seems to me a dangerous invasion by the state of the province of God's Church, however much it may have prevailed in the past or even been necessary to avoid a greater evil, such as a formal schism.

There is another practice which also ought to be avoided, I think, namely, the payment of the clergy's salaries by the government. Although not in itself an evil, it would easily and frequently lead to one or both of two great evils. First, by making the clergy financially dependent upon the state, it is apt to cause them to become subservient to the civil rulers, although as a matter of fact, the general tendency is for the clergy to be too uncritical in their acceptance of government policy, for example, on the question of the justice of a war. But if a situation occurred which required sharp comments on state policy, could one expect the clergy to (so to speak) bite the hand that fed them, or, on the part of the authorities, to subsidize their critics? The other evil which this would lead to would be a lessening of the sense of duty on the part of the laity toward supporting the Church with their gifts. I see nothing wrong, however, with the state supporting the Church from time to time with gifts for special purposes, such as construction of buildings, or a regular donation for the Church's charities or for education.

The second part of the application of Catholic doctrine on religious liberty concerns restrictions on non-Catholic worship and activity. The purpose of any restrictions imposed on such conduct is the protection of the common good of society, so it is not possible to lay down beforehand what should be done in this regard, except in the most general way, especially on the question of restricting the public worship of non-Catholics. It is easier, however, to consider the question of restrictions on proselytizing by non-Catholics. It seems to me that, wherever it would not cause greater harm, such as disruption of the civil order or the economy by a powerful and rich religious minority, or intervention by a foreign power sympathetic to a minority sect, that there should be a complete prohibition of all evangelizing activity by non-Catholic faiths. I cannot imagine that a Catholic state should ever take a lenient stance toward a practice that might result in even one Catholic being lost to the Church. Of course, despite everything, there will doubtless always be some personal attempts to proselytize by individuals here and there, and were the law to try to root out such it would bring about a tyranny. But any *organized* or *formal* attempts at seducing Catholics from the Faith that come to the notice of the authorities should not be permitted to continue. No doubt from time to time some Catholics will leave the Church, even with the best of laws, and this must be permitted as far as the civil law is concerned. Moreover, the members of a minority religion should not be penalized if Catholics join them, as long as they have done nothing to cause such defections from the Faith.[9]

Much harder to judge and to propose regulations for is the question of to what extent non-Catholics should be permitted to gather for worship and other religious activity, such as religious education. The question here concerns not only the possibility of Catholics leaving the Church or becoming indifferent to religious truth, but also of preserving a Catholic face to the public life of the nation. Now obviously non-Catholic

9 Naturally, what I say here and in the next section about non-Catholic religions applies also to secularists or unbelievers of any type.

religious gatherings would be permitted in private homes, and, it seems to me, that usually it would be wise to allow more than this. For example, to permit non-Catholic sects to have juridical personality, to own property, including buildings for worship and schools, as long as these buildings were not too prominent, imposing, etc., either as to form or location. If a Catholic culture is healthy, in the long run it must depend for its preservation on the strength of its Catholicism, not on suppression of other religions. But since the effect of original sin is an ever present reality, it is necessary to have restrictions on non-Catholic activity, yet it seems wiser in most cases to allow more, rather than less, freedom. Thus, also, if the state is not too harsh to a religious minority, more non-Catholics might consider conversion to the Catholic faith, than if they were subjected to too severe laws.

In estimating the requirements of the common good by means of the virtue of political prudence,[10] the rulers of the state should take account of the general tenor of the society, the degree of fervor and religious knowledge among Catholics, and the attitude commonly held toward members of minority religions by Catholics. If Catholics have a right regard for non-Catholics, having *truth in charity* toward them, then more religious freedom can be granted to those outside the Church. But if Catholics are ill-instructed and susceptible to being led into error, it may be that the activities of heretical sects and non-Christian religions should be kept entirely out of public sight and recognition, being confined to their private homes and unmarked church buildings. It is also possible that some false religions can be given more liberty than others, again, according to the requirements of the common good. For example, historical experience would say, I think, that it is relatively uncommon for Catholics to convert to

---

10   Cf. the *Catechism of the Catholic Church*, no. 2109.

Judaism; thus Jews could well be given more freedom than is given to heretical Christian sects, which experience shows can be great threats to a Catholic social order.

One other possibility that could obtain in some nations is that non-Catholics are well established only in some regions of the country. In such a case — one might think of the Waldenses in northern Italy — if they had a traditional or large presence there, the common good might dictate that they be able to exercise a larger degree of religious liberty there than in parts of the nation not infected with heresy. In fact, one can imagine the rulers of the state making a bargain with the leaders of the sect, allowing them greater exercise of religious freedom in certain restricted places in exchange for promises not to migrate to other parts of the country.

Another point to be considered is the question of non-Catholic activity by foreigners. It goes without saying that no non-Catholic missionaries would be permitted into a Catholic state, nor would foreign agencies be allowed to send money into the country for the purpose of undermining the Catholic social order in any way. Nor would the government be under any obligation to permit non-Catholics to enter the state to live there. The kind of religious minority we are looking at in this chapter is an indigenous one; the state has no duty, and indeed no right, to disturb the religious unity of a Catholic nation by allowing those of other religions, or of no religion, to come to live there.

What of aid supplied by foreign coreligionists to non-Catholic sects within a Catholic nation? Whether this should be permitted or not seems to me to depend on several factors. If the non-Catholic sect in question is a relatively benign one, both in terms of its own doctrines and practices, and in terms of how well its officials and members have obeyed the law against proselytizing, then the authorities might well permit aid from outside, for example, for new hymnbooks or textbooks. Could they ever allow a foreign pastor to come and serve a non-Catholic congregation? Again, as in the above example, if the false religion in question has a good record and there is a real need, I see no reason why not, though the authorities would have to take care that this neither is nor becomes a covert means of materially increasing the number of non-Catholics in the nation. But one or a few, including their families, would seem to make little difference. Such individuals could be given visas which allowed for easy deportation if trouble should arise.

If the state makes grants of money available to *parents* for the education of their children, it should not discriminate with regard to non-Catholics, even though it foresees that the money will be used to educate their children in heresy. The money is given to the parents for the legitimate purpose of education, and if the parents choose to misuse it, that is the right of the parents and does not implicate the state in the promotion of heresy.

In this discussion of religious liberty it is always important to remember, moreover, that only in countries overwhelmingly and traditionally Catholic would it be right to institute these kinds of restrictions on religious liberty, at least in their fullness. I see no reason why any Catholic government should be unable to honor Christ the King, even if it must permit full or considerable freedom to non-Catholic religious groups. But in order to restrict the activities of non-Catholics, I would argue that more is needed, namely, as I said, a society almost totally Catholic and traditionally so. For only in such cases does the state possess the necessary right to restrict non-Catholic activity. In addition, wherever even a very small religious minority has been allowed to function openly for a long space of time they acquire a kind of right by prescription. But the reader must remember that in this book I am dealing with abstract situations, and everything would have to be adapted to specific circumstances, keeping in mind justice, the common good and a Catholic sense, as judged by political prudence.

3

The Framework of Economic Activity

I

... if we have food and clothing, with these we shall be content. But those who desire to be rich fall into temptation, into a snare, into many senseless and hurtful desires that plunge men into ruin and destruction. For the love of money is the root of all evils; it is through this craving that some have wandered away from the faith and pierced their hearts with many pangs.   (I Tim. 6:8–10)

Come now, you rich, weep and howl for the miseries that are coming upon you. Your riches have rotted and your garments are moth-eaten. Your gold and silver have rusted, and their rust will be evidence against you and will eat your flesh like fire.
(James 5:1–3a)

FROM THESE AS WELL AS OTHER PASsages in both the Old and New Testaments[1] we ought to be able to see clearly that there is some sort of a problem in regard to riches and moneymaking. Quite obviously the problem is complex and cannot be reduced to saying that all the rich are evil and will end up in Hell nor that the desire for material goods is evil. Neither of these statements

---

1   Some other passages that tend toward the same point are: Proverbs 23:4; Micah 6:12a; Matthew 19:24; Luke 1:53b.

is true. Neither, however, can Christians accept the modern world's attitude toward riches and material things, an attitude which fails to see that there is anything to be troubled about. Catholicism, when it has been free to be true to itself, has always set up safeguards around the activities connected with money and the accumulation of wealth, safeguards for the common good and health of the community, as well as for the spiritual safety of the individual possessor of wealth himself, precisely because the Church knows the weakness of man and his propensity to sin.

Because of the original disaster that affects all of Adam's descendants, man tends to disorder, our appetites tend to revolt against our reason. We see this clearly in reference to our sexual appetites, but contemporary Catholics do not see this quite as clearly in regard to our appetite for pecuniary gain as did our medieval fathers in the Faith. Moreover, I think that we have not always well understood what it is about our sexual appetites that is disorderly. Some, I fear, have tended to see sexual desire as in a class by itself, either somehow inherently evil, or at least tainted. But this is not the correct way of looking at the matter, for the problem is not in our sexual desire itself, but in the entire integration of our human nature.

Man's sexual appetite and all that naturally goes with it were quite obviously created by God, and thus share in the original Divine approbation, "And God saw everything that he had made, and behold, it was very good," (Genesis 1:31).[2] They were created for a purpose, namely to bring new human beings into the world, and ultimately into Heaven, in cooperation with Almighty God. What is wrong with our sexual appetite today, and indeed since the Fall, is that the appetite tends toward objects with which it is impossible to obtain

2 See also *Summa Theologiae* I, q. 98, art. 2.

the end for which that appetite was given to us, that is, to beget children and bring up those children in the circle of a loving family. Our sexual desire, one of our concupiscible appetites, is indiscriminate and blind in its wants. Instead of being readily subordinate to its controlling purpose, the begetting and subsequent rearing of children, it simply wants what it wants. In the state of original justice the intellect easily ruled over all subordinate aspects of man, and thus would effortlessly have directed a person's sexual desire exclusively toward his spouse, but since Adam's sin this has not been the case. In our present condition we must all struggle to subject the concupiscible appetites to the rule of reason. But in this hard work of ruling our blind appetites we do not do anything against what is natural for us. We were created with reason as the ruling element in us and it is impossible to make sense of human beings in any other way; thus to restrain our blind desires within the bounds of reason, though at times a bitter effort, is simply to live as is natural to man, in fact, to live according to nature.

A similar thing is true of our desire for material things, which is the basis for our economic activity and all that goes with it. Since we have bodies we need material goods, and this would have been true had the Fall never occurred. But instead of asking why we need material things, we make them ends in themselves, not means toward allowing us to cultivate what is important in life, namely, our spiritual lives, our intellectual lives, our family and social lives. As with our sexual appetite, our desire for money and material goods is now more or less indiscriminate and inordinate in its wants. But also as with our sexual appetite, our appetite for material goods was created for an end. Material goods exist for the sake of the more important aspects of our lives. Such goods are good only to the extent that they facilitate our easier attainment or enjoyment of spiritual, intellectual, family and social goods, just as sexual activity is good to the extent it furthers one of the three ends of marriage.[3] And just as the sexual appetite run out of bounds will hurt not only the individuals involved but the entire community, the same is true of our appetite for economic gain. Adam Smith notwithstanding, it is not the case that if each of us seeks his own gain to the utmost the community will necessarily benefit thereby. History as well as common sense teach otherwise.[4]

One of the main reasons why this is so hard for many otherwise orthodox Catholics to grasp today is, I think, that we have been so accustomed to attacks on free-market capitalism coming from socialists and communists, that we assume only they can have anything bad to say about our economic

---

3 Compare the statement of Paul VI in the Encyclical *Populorum Progressio*, no. 19, "Increased possession is not the ultimate goal of nations nor of individuals. All growth is ambivalent. It is essential if man is to develop as a man, but in a way it imprisons man if he considers it the supreme good, and it restricts his vision. Then we see hearts harden and minds close, and men no longer gather together in friendship but out of self-interest, which soon leads to oppositions and disunity. The exclusive pursuit of possessions thus become an obstacle to individual fulfilment and to man's true greatness. Both for nations and for individual men, avarice is the most evident form of moral underdevelopment."

See also the *Catechism of the Catholic Church*, no. 2426.

4 This judgment is explicitly endorsed by Pius XI in *Quadragesimo Anno*, no. 88, " . . . the proper ordering of economic affairs cannot be left to the free play of rugged competition." This, I think, is the great stumbling block to many Catholics, at least in the United States, namely, acceptance of the notion that there must be both internal and external restraints on our economic appetite, including restraints enforced by the state or intermediary bodies, and that the satisfaction of this potentially boundless appetite is not always lawful.

John Paul II's encyclical, *Centesimus Annus*, though widely hailed as a paean to the free market, is equally emphatic about the need for juridical restraints to orient economic activity toward the common good. See especially nos. 35, 40, 42 and 48.

system. But just as the logic of looking at our sexual appetite and the role it ought to play in human affairs according to its own nature leads us to conclude that man must put many restraints on his sexual conduct, which at the time feel as if they were going against his nature, but in reality are fulfilling that nature, in a similar fashion, if we ask ourselves fundamental questions about man's capacity for and need of material goods, and look honestly at the disruptive effect unrestrained economic activity has on human society, we are led to propose strong curbs, curbs which indeed are often different from those proposed by socialists, but which are equally contrary to our present system and to the desires of unrestrained greed.

If any Catholic is disposed to dispute this line of argument, then I would point out two different things which confirm what I have said. The first is the practice of medieval Christendom. The attitude toward economic activity that obtained in Europe during the Middle Ages was vastly different from our own. The following from Richard Tawney conveys some idea of the medieval outlook:

> Material riches are necessary; they have a secondary importance, since without them men cannot support themselves and help one another; the wise ruler, as St. Thomas said, will consider in founding his State the natural resources of the country. But economic motives are suspect. Because they are powerful appetites, men fear them, but they are not mean enough to applaud them. Like other strong passions, what they need, it is thought, is not a clear field, but repression. There is no place in medieval theory for economic activity which is not related to a moral end, and to found a science of society upon the assumption that the appetite

for economic gain is a constant and measurable force, to be accepted, like other natural forces, as an inevitable and self-evident *datum* would have appeared to the medieval thinker as hardly less irrational or less immoral than to make the premise of social philosophy the unrestrained operation of such necessary human attributes as pugnacity or the sexual instinct.

Tawney continues with his description of medieval economic ethics,

At every turn, therefore, there are limits, restrictions, warnings, against allowing economic interests to interfere with serious affairs. It is right for a man to seek such wealth as is necessary for a livelihood in his station. To seek more is not enterprise, but avarice, and avarice is a deadly sin. Trade is legitimate; the different resources of different countries show that it was intended by Providence. But it is a dangerous business. A man must be sure that he carries it on for the public benefit, and that the profits which he takes are no more than the wages of his labor.[5]

How unbelievably different is our modern attitude. With us not only is trade in goods no longer held to be a dangerous activity, but we see no problem even in trade in such nebulous things as futures contracts! It is difficult to fully fathom the huge differences in our mentality from that of the medievals. Most English-speaking Catholics are infected to a greater or lesser extent with the modern and unchristian conception of economic life. Christopher Dawson sums up this modern attitude thus:

---

5   Richard H. Tawney, *Religion and the Rise of Capitalism*, pp. 31–32.

In the lands where these [new, non-Catholic] ideals
had free play — Holland, Great Britain, above all
New England, a new type of character was produced, canny, methodical and laborious; men who
lived not for enjoyment but for work, who spent
little and gained much, and who looked on themselves as unfaithful stewards before God, if they
neglected any opportunity of honest gain.[6]

The second thing to which I would appeal in confirmation of this line of argument is the corpus of modern papal
teaching on the economy. As is well known, this body of
doctrine began with the encyclical *Rerum Novarum* of Leo
XIII in 1891, and has continued into the pontificate of Pope
Francis. Though diverse, in that the popes were for the most
part addressing the immediate needs of widely varying situations — the economy of 1891 is not that of 1931 nor yet that of
today — nevertheless several basic themes can be discerned.[7]

From the beginning, with *Rerum Novarum*, the Popes
have made it clear that the economic system must serve
mankind, and from this it follows that any particular economic arrangements must be judged on how well they in
fact are serving the human race.[8] Secondly, they have also
pointed out again and again that it will always be necessary
to bring other factors into the ordering of our economic
affairs besides mere free competition. Some kind of legal

---

6 "Economics in the Medieval and in the Modern World," *The Dawson Newsletter*, vol. 3, no. 4 (winter 1984–85), p. 3. (Reprinted from
Blackfriars, July 1924.)

7 For a summary and commentary on these encyclicals and related
documents, see my book, *An Economics of Justice and Charity: Catholic Social Teaching, Its Development and Contemporary Relevance*,
(Angelico Press, 2017).

8 Cf. *Rerum Novarum*, nos. 7–8, 22, 35; *Quadragesimo Anno*, nos.
43 and 75; *Laborem Exercens*, no. 10; *Centesimus Annus*, nos. 30–31, 53.

framework is necessary to make sure that economic affairs truly serve the common good. One cannot depend either on the blind forces of the market or enlightened self-interest or even individual rectitude.[9]

Now the purpose of the restraints on economic activity which this attitude demands is twofold. On the one hand, if the activities of moneymaking and the accumulation of external goods are firmly put in their place, mankind will be able to concentrate more easily on what is really of importance in life. Men of good will, who in a capitalistic economy and society might devote too much of their energies to material things and even get entirely caught up in them, will be deterred from this not only by the explicit teaching of the Church, but also by regulations of both the state and of intermediate groups, which aim to prevent the beginnings of wrongdoing in these matters. These same regulations, on the other hand, backed by appropriate sanctions, will also help to forestall the actions of truly bad men, who would otherwise harm their fellows and the society as a whole.

Though no one can expect this apparatus to work perfectly, its aim is to uphold the common good and to reinforce an understanding of society in which private gain is subordinated to the general welfare. Christopher Dawson noted that the traditional monarchies in Europe "had striven to keep the several orders of the polity within their appointed limits, to maintain the corporative system in industry, to regulate wages and prices, and to protect the peasants from eviction and enclosures."[10] This conception of society does not espe-

---

9   See, for example, *Rerum Novarum*, nos. 26–29, 33–34; *Quadragesimo Anno*, nos. 25–28, 49, 61, 76–96; *Populorum Progressio*, nos. 58–61; *Centesimus Annus*, nos. 35, 40, 42, 48.

10   "The Historic Origins of Liberalism" in *The Image of Man* (Notre Dame: University of Notre Dame, 1959), p. 110.

cially value some notions that are dear to Americans, such as continuous improvement in one's standard of living or the chance to get rich. But it does aim to allow everyone to have at least enough, and to further ensure the maintenance of that social peace which is necessary if we are to apply ourselves to those things which are truly important. For if material goods exist only for the sake of non-material ends, and if money in turn exists only for the sake of material goods, then money is twice removed from what is valuable in human life. But how a Catholic state actually tries to realize such an approach to living is the subject of the following sections of this chapter.

II

> We can, therefore, lay down as the first principle of mediaeval economics that there was a limit to money-making imposed by the purpose for which the money was made. Each worker had to keep in front of himself the aim of his life and consider the acquiring of money as a means only to an end, which at one and the same time justified and limited him. When, therefore, sufficiency had been obtained there could be no reason for continuing further efforts at getting rich, . . . except in order to help others. . . . [11]   — Fr. Bede Jarrett

In considering actual institutions and policies to realize such a Christian order as I sketched out in the preceding section, it is necessary first to discuss in some more detail the basic principles which both the supreme pontiffs have taught and which were actually put into place by medieval Christendom, and which reflected the truths about man's

---

[11] *Social Theories of the Middle Ages* (Westminster, Md.: Newman, 1942) pp. 157–158.

economic appetite which I discussed above. And in beginning, it again must be stressed that all the social doctrine of the Church and the social practice of Catholics is related to a recognition of the purpose of economic activity. To take up the same analogy I used before, if there is no intrinsic purpose in our sexual desire, then each individual is surely justified in fulfilling such desire for whatever reason, and in whatever way, he wishes. On this view, sexual desire or sexual activity as a whole is purposeless; it is only each person's own sexual activity which has a purpose, and that purpose is whatever he chooses to give to it. This line of argument, of course, justifies limitless and irresponsible indulgence in sex, and perhaps even the violence of rape or sadism, if that is what pleases someone, for who am I to say that my desires are better than yours? No, to judge something, to pronounce that something is objectively better or worse, it is necessary to have some standard greater than mere individual predilection, in fact, an inherent purpose. If this is the case, then it is up to us to conform to that purpose, which in fact will be what is truly natural for us, and, to the extent we fail to do so, our behavior is blameworthy. If any human activity has its own purpose, apart from the desires of this or that person, then our individual behavior must always be subordinated to that purpose, and evaluated on how well it in fact fulfills that purpose.

The purpose of our economic activity, as we saw above, is simply to facilitate man's spiritual, intellectual, family and social life, by making available the material goods and services we need.[12] Any arrangement of economic activity is good only to the extent it contributes to that purpose. If it

---

12 Fr. Jarrett (*Social Theories of the Middle Ages*) quotes St. Thomas and St. Antoninus on the subordination of moneymaking to the inherent purpose of wealth. See pp. 154–156.

hinders that purpose, then it is bad and must be reformed. Economic activity is not something autonomous, existing simply with its own laws, to which everything else must adapt. If a particular economic structure is making family life difficult, then it is not family life that must adapt, but rather the economic structure must be changed. If, for example, factories are closing, forcing people to move, breaking up long-established neighborhoods and extended families, it is not enough just to say that that's how it is, and that we must go along with the economic system or with the supposed sacred rights of business, etc. No, for the entire economic system exists only for the sake of individuals and families. If it is not serving them, then it has lost its title to exist, and must be changed. It is true that one cannot make bricks without straw, and no amount of sermons on social justice can make the impossible possible.[13] But there should never be any question as to who should yield, business or the family, when there is conflict between them.

If this is so, it should be clear that no economic system can be oriented toward the true common good except by means of a juridical framework, that is, a set of laws, regulations and institutions designed to point economic activity toward its true end. Pius XI is quite explicit about the need for such laws. In *Quadragesimo Anno* he wrote the following:

---

13   Pius XI had the following to say in *Quadragesimo Anno*, no. 42. "For, though economic activity and moral discipline are guided each by its own principles in its own sphere, it is false that the two orders are so distinct and alien that the former in no way depends on the latter. The laws of economics, as they are called, derived from the nature of earthly goods and from the qualities of the human body and soul, determine what aims are unattainable or attainable in economic matters and what means are thereby necessary. But reason itself clearly deduces from the nature of things and from the individual and social character of man, what is the end and object of the whole economic order assigned by God the Creator."

It is therefore very necessary that economic affairs be once more subjected to and governed by a true and effective guiding principle.... It cannot, however, be curbed and governed by itself. More lofty and noble principles must therefore be sought in order to regulate this supremacy firmly and honestly: to wit, social justice and social charity.

To that end all the institutions of public and social life must be imbued with the spirit of justice, and this justice must above all be truly operative. It must build up a juridical and social order able to pervade all economic activity. Social charity should be, as it were, the soul of this order. It is the duty of the State to safeguard effectively and to vindicate promptly this order....   (no. 88)[14]

Laws are needed, not only because of the propensity of fallen humanity to mistreat each other—*homo homini lupus*—man is a wolf to man—but because some sort of ordering principle is needed in any society. The important question, of course, is exactly what will be those laws that will curb and govern the economic order. After all, communism attempted to do that, ostensibly in the interests of the poor and the common good. What will be the Catholic legal framework of economic justice, especially as it would exist in an explicitly Catholic regime? Broadly speaking, such a framework will contain the following elements: first, as Pius XI noted, social justice and social charity spread throughout the entire social order; secondly and more specifically, a recognition of the essential harmony of the interests of all classes in society, a correct understanding of the right and purpose of private property, and a thoroughgoing application of the principle of subsidiarity, which necessarily includes the

---

14   See also the references given above in note 9.

recognition and organization of occupational groups. Let us look at each of these points in more detail.

The classical definition of justice is "to render to each man his due," and social justice necessarily has regard to this just rendering as it involves the very structures of society, i.e., just laws and policies, well-functioning groups and institutions, and so on, all of which will tend to promote justice by their very natures and relationships. This is not to say, as we shall see later, that institutions and structures by themselves can guarantee virtue — only that they are an indispensable aid and framework.

How is all this to be applied concretely, especially under a system of wages? At the very beginning of *Quadragesimo Anno* Pius XI speaks of the situation at the end of the nineteenth century, when many Catholics looked on the "undeserved misery of the laboring classes, and . . . could not persuade themselves that so vast and unfair a distinction in the distribution of temporal goods was really in harmony with the designs of an all-wise Creator" (no. 5). In other words, simply the presence of so much misery on the one hand and so much superfluous wealth on the other, seems to be enough evidence to convince the Pope that this is not in accord with justice, particularly with the truth that "the earth, though divided among private owners, ceases not thereby to minister to the needs of all . . . " (*Rerum Novarum*, no. 7). One cannot justify that grossly unequal arrangement by arguing that the workingmen were not able to produce sufficient of economic value to obtain higher wages or that, after all, they had freely accepted a low rate of pay. No, for justice simply demands that all men be treated as human persons, and as such, each should receive his due.

In *Quadragesimo Anno* Pius XI treats extensively of justice, and in this context notes the demand of *commutative* justice, the most strict kind,[15] that the wage earner receive at least a living family wage, "the wage paid to the workingman should be sufficient for the support of himself and of his family" (no. 71). A few pages later he says that this wage should allow the worker to obtain material goods

> sufficient to supply all needs and an honest live-
> lihood, and to uplift men to that higher level of
> prosperity and culture which, provided it be used
> with prudence, is not only no hindrance but is of
> singular help to virtue.   (no. 75).[16]

These are the minimum demands of justice under the system in which the owners of capital are normally separate from those who do the actual work in a concern (cf. *Quadragesimo Anno*, nos. 100-101).[17] But granting that this system is morally acceptable, one may ask whether it is an ideal

---

15   See also *Divini Redemptoris*, no. 49. On the various types of justice, see the *Catechism of the Catholic Church*, no. 2411.

16   "Employers ordinarily are bound under an obligation of Commutative Justice to give their employees a wage sufficient for the support of the worker and his family in becoming conditions. The worker's right to such a just wage is prior to the capitalist's claim to a dividend on his investments. Hence the employer or capitalist owner cannot justly appropriate from the industry anything more than a just wage for his own personal labour until the claims of the worker to a just wage are satisfied." Cahill, *The Framework of a Christian State*, p. 398.

17   I consider this to be the best definition of capitalism, namely, that given in *Quadragesimo Anno*, no. 100, as "that economic system in which were provided by different people the capital and labor jointly needed for production." Now, the actual historical "spirit of capitalism" is something more than this, something definitely contrary to Christian teaching and social justice. Seldom has capitalism operated in a benign way. Moreover, I would argue that even if it did, it would still not be the best arrangement for a Catholic society, or for any society for that matter. Ownership and labor are best when not separated. This point will be taken up in more detail later. On the question of Pius XI's definition of capitalism, see Oswald von Nell-Breuning, *Reorganization of Social Economy* (Milwaukee: Bruce, c. 1936–37), p. 270.

arrangement. Later we will take up the question in detail of what is the ideal economic pattern for a Catholic society, but at this point I will simply point out that nearly all the social encyclicals urge more extensive property ownership on the part of workers, suggesting that the Pontiffs themselves do not regard the separation between worker and capital as exactly the ideal.[18]

Proceeding to the next major point, Pius XI termed social charity the soul of a just social order, and it is important to realize that no set of external arrangements can guarantee justice for all. This is part of the reason why simply changing structures cannot bring about social justice, because justice, especially when framed into laws, can never accurately foresee every situation and can even be administered in a harsh and unyielding manner. In *Hamlet* Polonius says he will treat the visiting actors "according to their desert." Hamlet replies,

> God's bodykins, man, much better. Use every man
> after his desert, and who shall scape whipping?
>
> (II, 2)

Though justice is obviously essential for a society, nevertheless to be fixated on it alone will often lead to harshness. In *Dives in Misericordia*, John Paul II wrote,

> And yet, it would be difficult not to notice that very
> often programs which start from the idea of justice
> and which ought to assist its fulfillment among
> individuals, groups and human societies, in practice
> suffer from distortions. Although they continue to
> appeal to the idea of justice, nevertheless experience
> shows that other negative forces have gained the

---

18   For encyclical teachings on widespread ownership, see the following: *Rerum Novarum*, nos. 4 and 35; *Quadragesimo Anno*, nos. 59 to 63; *Mater et Magistra*, nos. 112 to 115; *Laborem Exercens*, no. 14.

> upper hand over justice, such as spite, hatred and
> even cruelty. (no. 12)

Justice that is not filled with a constant reference to charity, and even to mercy, can be a fearsome power which can seem to be zealously working for a kind of abstract righteousness that does not care about the fate of individual men. Justice will be all the more true to itself if it is coupled with charity.[19]

It is often assumed, more or less unconsciously today, that the interests of the different classes or groups in society are opposed to one another, for example, that the interests of producers and consumers, farmers and urban dwellers, and especially, of workers and managers or owners, are contradictory. But the direct opposite of this, particularly with regard to labor and management, is strongly insisted upon in papal social teaching.[20] Aside from the authoritative teaching of the papal magisterium on this subject, it is easy from reason alone to see why this must be the case. For if God is the author of all, including of civil society, could he have placed at the heart of things a necessary conflict between the various groups into which the human race is divided? Even granting that it is not ideal for capital and labor to be separated as they are in the capitalistic system, and that in a sense this system is a disease and degeneration of a healthy state, still society is a natural and therefore God-given state for man, and all of us have common interests. This point will be discussed further in the section dealing with occupational groups.

---

19 On social charity see also *Quadragesimo Anno*, no. 137. On the limits of justice see, Josef Pieper, *The Four Cardinal Virtues*, p. 112. In *Centesimus Annus* Pope John Paul equates social charity with the virtue or "principle of solidarity" (no. 10). See also Benedict XVI, encyclical *Caritas in Veritate*, nos. 1–7.

20 See especially *Rerum Novarum*, no. 15; *Quadragesimo Anno*, nos. 81 to 87.

In discussing social justice, labor and the ownership of capital, the institution of private property has been assumed. But it is necessary to discuss this in more detail, both because it is a bedrock of the social order and because errors of different kinds have long affected men's minds on this subject. In the first place, one must ask, since private property is a right, what is the purpose of that right? Rights are not given for no purpose at all, but rather to accomplish some end, and the right to private property is no exception. Surprisingly, this right is given so as to efficiently and peaceably make available to all the fruits of the earth. That is, the earth was given for the sustenance of the entire human race, and the institution of private property is simply the best means to accomplish that sustenance.[21] Therefore, if any particular arrangement of private property is not accomplishing that purpose, it must be changed. For though the right to property is from God and the interrelated system of natures which he created, the specific right of property can take many forms, as Pius XI noted,[22] and the civil law can rightly determine, within the wide bounds of the natural law, the limits and forms of this right. The state, to be sure, does not have the right to abolish private property, but it can regulate its forms in order to better provide for the very purpose for which property exists. For example, in the Middle Ages, guild regulations, backed by the civil law, in many places limited the number of apprentices each master could employ, thus limiting how far each could expand his own business. The purpose of this was to safeguard the common good by preventing one owner from acquiring too much property and putting others out

---

21   Cf. *Rerum Novarum*, nos. 6 to 8; *Quadragesimo Anno*, nos. 45 to 52, 114–115; *Mater et Magistra*, nos. 108 to 115; *Populorum Progressio*, nos. 22 to 24; *Laborem Exercens*, no. 14; *Centesimus Annus*, no. 31. See also, St. Thomas Aquinas, *Summa Theologiae* II–II, q. 66, art. 2.
22   *Quadragesimo Anno*, no. 49.

of business. For when one owner acquires more property than he needs for the support of himself and his family, any additional property he obtains is necessarily at someone else's expense, thus making it less easy for the earth's goods to support the entire human race, since some have appropriated for themselves more than they need. In addition, this tends to create social instability, unemployment and the beginnings of a permanent proletariat class.[23]

The last general principle that must be mentioned before we discuss their actual application is the principle of subsidiarity. This principle was originally stated by Pius XI in *Quadragesimo Anno* as follows:

---

23 John A. Ryan, *Distributive Justice* 3rd ed. (New York: Macmillan, 1942) p. 224, states explicitly that the state may limit the quantity and kind of property one may own. "There is nothing in the nature of things nor in the purpose of property to indicate that the right of ownership is unlimited in quantity any more than it is in quality. The final end and justification of individual rights of property is human welfare; that is, the welfare of all individuals severally and collectively."

Fanfani, *Catholicism, Protestantism and Capitalism*, pp. 50–51, mentions some of the restrictions on the use of property imposed by the medieval guilds on their members.

In the Middle Ages much property in land was not individually owned, but was owned in common. For example, the so-called "medieval open field" was a situation in which villages held land in common and allotted its use, some for individual use, some for common use, such as grazing. An interesting discussion of property rights, which focuses on common ownership, including family ownership, is Robert C. Ellickson, "Property in Land," *Yale Law Journal*, vol. 102, no. 6, April 1993, pp. 1315–1395. The account of the medieval open field is on pages 1388–1394.

Fr. Jarrett, *Social Theories of the Middle Ages*, pp. 133–149, discusses medieval notions of land tenure, arguing that in the Middle Ages land was never owned, but merely "held" in exchange for duties to be performed by the tenant — whether this was a nobleman or a serf.

The point of this is not that cooperative ownership is always better, but that it sometimes is, and unlike the Lockean ideologue, a Catholic should be willing to evaluate different types of property ownership on their merits.

> ... it is a fundamental principle of social philosophy, fixed and unchangeable, that one should not withdraw from individuals and commit to the community what they can accomplish by their own enterprise and industry. So, too, it is an injustice and at the same time a grave evil and a disturbance of right order, to transfer to the larger and higher collectivity functions which can be performed and provided for by lesser and subordinate bodies. Inasmuch as every social activity should, by its very nature, prove a help to members of the body social, it should never destroy or absorb them. (no. 79)

The principle stated here is a key to understanding how Catholic teaching transcends the sterile debate between what we in the United States call the Right and the Left, on the role of the state in the economy. For as will be made clearer in the discussion of occupational groups in the next section, the framing and enforcement of regulations for the sake of the common good is often naturally lodged elsewhere than in the central government. To take a humble example, the enforcement of the common good in a family is naturally lodged in the parents. This is not a right and duty delegated to them by the state; it is their right and duty in the nature of things. Similarly the enforcement of the common good within a town or an industry is not naturally the province directly of the central government either. Those who are closer to the situation itself, those who inhabit the town or who work in the industry, are both more familiar with the situation and its exigencies and better able to take care of them. We are more likely to be able to understand this truth without hesitation in regard to local government, and it is only with difficulty that we apply it to the economy. But the application of this principle of subsidiarity is, I think, the most revolutionary aspect of Catholic teaching on economic morality.[24]

How exactly will a Catholic state frame its laws so as to accomplish all these points? That is the subject of the last two sections of this chapter.

III

> At one period there existed a social order which, though by no means perfect in every respect, corresponded nevertheless in a certain measure to right reason according to the needs and conditions of the times.
>
> — Pope Pius XI, *Quadragesimo Anno*, no. 97

In this and the next section of this chapter I will discuss the specific institutions which Catholic social thought suggests are necessary in order to apply the principles which were treated of above. And undoubtedly the chief institution and the key to having a just economy, which at the same time avoids the errors of statism, is an institution sometimes called an occupational group, or more commonly, a guild.[25]

---

24 The principle of subsidiarity has been applied by Catholics to the economy since the encyclical *Quadragesimo Anno*. This far-reaching principle can also, I think, be applied to cultural creation and dissemination, and I have argued this point in *The Catholic Milieu*, (Christendom College 1987), pp. 43–49, and in "When Small is Sensible: Culture, Technology and Subsidiarity," *Caelum et Terra*, vol. I, no. 2, fall 1991.

25 In addition to guild, occupational groups have been called by various names, including the following: vocational groups, functional groups, industry councils, organized industries and professions, corporations, professional bodies, orders, estates. See Raymond J. Miller, *Forty Years After: Pius XI and the Social Order* (St. Paul, Minn.: Frs. Rumble & Carty, c. 1947), pp. 161–62, for a discussion of the best English name for these bodies.

Although the concept of the occupational group is little known or comprehended today, especially in the United States, its importance for a right understanding of the subject of the economy can hardly be overstated.[26] Such groups are the chief way to avoid the errors of, on the one hand, direct state control of the economy, or, on the other, of allowing free competition to be the ruling principle of economic affairs. Both of these approaches are wrong, and the occupational group is the means to escape them. The reason that either statism or the free market seems like the only solution to the problem of economic regulation is that most people have accepted uncritically the notion that there is only one body which can rightly intervene on behalf of the common good with the force of law. And this body, of course, is the state. Thus some, anxious to avoid the manifest injustices that result from the rule of the free market, propose more or less massive regulation by the central state authorities. And others, reacting against the evils and economic absurdities that can come from such regulation, offer again the free market. Is there no escape from this conflict? There *is* an escape, and it is not a middle way of a small amount of regulation, just

In 1948 a committee of the American Catholic Sociological Society recommended the term "industry council," and the American bishops, in a statement later that year, took note of that decision. John F. Cronin, *Catholic Social Principles* (Milwaukee: Bruce, 1950) pp. 221–22. However, I prefer the term *occupational group* as being more generic.
26   It is sometimes asserted that papal documents after Pius XII no longer recommend or mention occupational groups, leading some to suppose that they are not to be considered a permanent part of Catholic social doctrine. However, this is not the case. *Mater et Magistra* refers to them (no. 37), and later speaks of the necessary activities of intermediate groups (see nos. 65–67, 84, 86–90, 100). John Paul II also clearly alludes to occupational groups in *Laborem Exercens.*, nos. 14 and 20. See also *Centesimus Annus*, nos. 7, 13, 43, 48, and Benedict XVI's criticism of the "binary model of market-plus-State" in *Caritas in Veritate*, nos. 39 and 41.

the right amount. Aside from the fact that we could never agree on exactly how much was appropriate, a little bit of regulation leaves numerous injustices uncorrected, while at the same time giving the state a taste and precedent for intervention whenever there is a problem that no one else is presently addressing. No, the solution involves applying the principle of subsidiarity and recognizing and giving form to the naturally existing occupational groups.

The principle of subsidiarity — the principle that higher and larger bodies, including the state, should not take over the legitimate functions and duties of lower and smaller ones — is the key to dealing successfully with the socio-economic question, because it allows regulation of the economy in the interests of justice and protection of workers and consumers, yet without the immediate presence of the machinery of central government. And it does this, not by *delegating* the right to regulate to smaller and lower bodies, but by allowing the powers of regulation that naturally lodge in smaller groups to be exercised without hindrance, subject only to general supervision by the state, by way of "directing, supervising, encouraging, restraining"[27] should one of the lower bodies require such.[28]

---

27   Pius XI, Encyclical *Quadragesimo Anno*, no. 80. Although Leo XIII in *Rerum Novarum* (nos. 36–43) had mentioned and recommended the establishment of organizations which were to have some of the functions of occupational groups, it is Pius XI who for the first time delineates the occupational group proper. His classic account of their nature and functions is in *Quadragesimo Anno*, nos. 81 to 87.

28   The liberal mind has difficulty conceiving that such authority can rightly belong to any entity except the state. See, for example, James Q. Whitman, "Of Corporatism, Fascism, and the First New Deal," *American Journal of Comparative Law*, vol. 39, no. 4, fall 1991, pp. 747–778. On p. 752 he says, "Nevertheless, elusive as 'corporatism' may be, all orders identified by social scientists as 'corporatist' share,

Now the lower and smaller bodies that I am concerned with here are, of course, the occupational groups. And the best way to introduce them is to show that, far from being a layer of bureaucracy created by European clerics and ideologues, they are naturally existing groups, and an economy such as that of the United States, where they are unorganized and unrecognized, is an unnatural economy.

When people have a common task to accomplish and are engaged upon that task, *ipso facto*, simply by virtue of their common task, they form a separate and special group set apart for that task. Perhaps they do not realize this fact, and perhaps the group is unorganized and unacknowledged, but nonetheless it exists. Consider twenty men, occupied in digging a ditch. They form a group because of their collective work and purpose. The relations among them are, or at least should be, governed by their mutual connections with the work being performed. The more this is recognized and accepted, the better and faster will the work be finished. In fact, if they refuse to allow that their common task imposes any kind of unity on them, that is, if they will not acknowledge that the work itself has created a unity, then they are not likely to dig a ditch at all, but twenty separate holes instead. The point to be noted here is that, in so far as the workmen are aiming at a common end, they have a unity arising from the work itself; it is not a unity artificially

---

to the eye of any American lawyer, one feature: they involve the *delegation* of what most lawyers think of as state powers to private organizations. Accordingly, for purposes of this paper, I will define 'corporatism' as the delegation of powers that, in a given society, are generally considered *state* powers, to *private* organizations."

To the liberal mind, whatever is not governmental is private, and private in the sense of voluntary and not necessary for the common good. This kind of thinking is characteristic of liberals of all types, including those known in the United States as *conservatives*.

imposed on them from the outside. It is a natural unity, in view of and because of the shared work. This is true, moreover, whether the twenty are employees of the same firm, separate independent contractors or even volunteers. And this unity extends also to anyone who may be giving the actual diggers instructions or direction in their effort. He too is part of this common work.

In the encyclical letter *Quadragesimo Anno* (no. 87) Pope Pius XI compares this unity arising from shared work to that arising from proximity of dwelling. People living in the same town have a unity among themselves based on their geographical nearness. The town government simply expresses and orders this existing unity, it does not create it. The inhabitants of the town naturally come together to solve their common problems — police and fire protection, sanitation, infrastructure, and so on, and generally form structured bodies to deal more effectively with these problems: local governments, volunteer fire departments, property owner associations, community leagues, and the like. But the important thing to note is that unless there were an already existing unity, natural and not artificially created or imposed, the people could hardly organize for themselves formal instruments, such as governments, to express that unity. Both the common problems and the bodies created to solve the problems can exist only because geography has made a unity. Of course, this unity need not incline them to cooperate, for it is a unity of geographical proximity, not necessarily of attitude and will. But it does make such cooperation both possible and natural. It is a necessary condition for it.

Can factors other than geographical proximity create such unity? Above I illustrated a unity based on an immediate shared task, that of digging a ditch. But can this be carried further? Take, for example, all the bakers and bakeries in one nation. Though they might have little geographical near- ness or unity arising from a physically shared joint task, yet because they are all engaged in one kind of work, they do have a unity based on common concerns and aims. They are all interested, for example, in price and availability of their raw materials, in new technologies, in ability to obtain skilled workers. They likewise exhibit their unity in their collective concern over questions of marketing, such as price of their product, market share of the various establishments, their relations with governmental bodies, etc. In short, they have similar problems and interests resulting from their com- mon work.

Thus it is easy to see that there is a natural unity even among widely scattered producers of the same product or ser- vice, and that, to be effective in dealing with common needs and problems, this unity should be embodied in a formal organization.[29] The industry or trade association is expressive of a part of this unity of individuals and firms engaged in the same kind of work. But there is another aspect to the unity of those doing the same work. This is the unity between employer and employed, and is interestingly illustrated in a

---

29 The grocery industry in the U. S. adopted bar coding cooper- atively and voluntarily: "... in mid-1970, an industry consortium established an ad hoc committee to look into bar codes. The com- mittee set guidelines for bar-code development and created a sym- bol-selection subcommittee to help standardize the approach." The chairman of the subcommittee was quoted as saying, "We showed that it could be done on a massive scale, that cooperation without antitrust implications was possible for the common good, and that business didn't need the government to shove it in the right direc- tion." Tony Seideman, "Bar Codes Sweep the World," *Invention & Technology*, vol. 8, no. 4, spring 1993, p. 60. There is no reason why such a cooperative approach among businesses could not be the norm instead of the exception.

passage from John Steinbeck's novel of the 1930s, *The Grapes of Wrath*. In the book a labor contractor is recruiting men at one of the numerous migrant camps in California. The recruiter is vague about the conditions of work, including the rate of wages. The following dialogue ensues:

> Floyd stepped out ahead. He said quietly, "I'll go, mister. You're a contractor, an' you got a license. You jus' show your license, an' then you give us an order to go to work, an' where, an' when, an' how much we'll get, an' you sign that, an' we'll all go."
>
> The contractor turned, scowling. "You telling me how to run my own business?"
>
> Floyd said, "'F we're workin' for you, it's our business too."

This last line, "'F we're workin' for you, it's our business too," expresses exactly the truth that in a real sense the business belongs to all who work for it, whether legally owners or not, because all who work for it are legitimately concerned about profits, working conditions, prospects for the future, since all of these people must draw their livelihood and their families' livelihood from it. If a firm or an entire industry is declining, no matter what the reason, it is absurd to imagine that only the owners or managers should worry, on the grounds that only they are legally responsible for such questions. As if the workers should peacefully go on welding pipes or working their computers till the day their paychecks cease! The truth is that everyone, worker, manager or owner, will, or should, prosper if the firm prospers, and everyone will suffer if the firm suffers. Especially the workers.

That there is no natural antipathy between employer and employee, but rather a unity based on their shared work and common fortune, is one of the points insisted on most strongly in papal social thought, as well as in the perceptive comments of many others.[30] When an industry comes upon hard times, it is not uncommon for all involved to contribute to efforts to keep the industry prosperous. We fail to see that such temporary collaboration ought to be the norm. The obvious fact is that both labor and management must draw their living from the same source, the sale of the products or services they jointly provide. They both depend on each

---

30   People are always rediscovering for themselves the truths taught in the Church's social encyclicals. See for example, *Labor-Management Cooperation: 1990 State-of-the-Art Symposium*, published by the Bureau of Labor-Management Relations and Cooperative Programs of the U. S. Dept. of Labor in 1991. This is a summary of a conference held by the Bureau on restructuring companies in order to achieve a situation in which labor and management have "an equal stake and an equal say in the success of the organization" (p. 1). The entire book is replete with insights and suggestions that the Roman Pontiffs had decades ago, even to the point of shared ownership (p. 42) and the fact that both the union and management often have a common point of view on dealing with the "external environment—lobbying the government on tariffs and other issues vital to an entire industry..." (p. 26).

In Germany what is called "codetermination," an organized system of cooperation between workers and management, was established beginning in 1951. The German attitude can be summed up as follows:

> Employers' associations and trade unions do not see themselves as opponents but as partners in an agreement that forms the basis of the economic development of the country. Each side is fully aware that it is dependent upon the other. Both know that at the end of negotiations, agreement must be reached. Furthermore, both sides affirm their responsibility for finding solutions to existing social problems. This results in a basic consensus that is not destroyed by occasional industrial disputes. For this reason, employers' organizations and trade unions in Germany are usually referred to as *social partners*.

Under codetermination, the chief board of a German industrial concern is comprised of "an equal number of shareholders' representatives and employees' representatives...." Uwe Liebig, "Dialogue Instead of Confrontation: the German System," *Canada-U. S. Outlook*, vol. 3, no. 4, May 1993, pp. 56–57. Thus one of the major economic powers in the world openly applies a central tenet of Catholic teaching!

other, and both have a natural interest in perfecting their joint productive work in order to obtain the greatest prosperity for the industry, and thus for themselves.

If one argues that labor and management are naturally in competition for their share of the return they make from sales, why are the laborer and the company president more in competition than the company vice-presidents and the president? It is true that out of a finite amount the compensation of the managers cannot be increased indefinitely without there being less for the workers to receive. But likewise, the compensation of the president cannot be increased without limit without there being less for the vice-presidents to receive. Yet no one thinks of the latter as being naturally at war with the president. No, the supposed naturalness of industrial warfare, between owners and managers on the one side, and workers on the other, does not arise from the nature of production, or even from the factory system,[31] but is a peculiar state of affairs, brought into being by human greed, fueled by the lack of ethical ideals in our economic system, and the disparity in power and prestige between employers and workers. Industrial warfare is not natural and need not be permanent.

The unity which is brought about by making the same product or providing the same service extends to all involved in the work, regardless of position on the labor market. An organization comprising all such, that is, which includes employers, employees, and owner-operators is what is meant by an occupational group. Such groups simply express and order the natural unity that already exists between all engaged in the same productive process, and allows those so engaged to more easily accomplish their common ends.

---

31 "Opposition between labor and capital does not spring from the structure of the production process or from the structure of the economic process." John Paul II, encyclical *Laborem Exercens*, no. 13.

What are the occupational group's ends, its purposes and functions? Their first function, as I suggested above, is to unite all who labor in the same industry or profession to advance their common interests. An occupational group would obviously take an interest in both internal and external aspects of the industry, that is, relations among various subgroups within the industry, the industry's relations with suppliers, consumers, the government, etc. In short, the occupational group would attempt to coordinate all involved in the work to keep full the common pot out of which all must be fed, particularly striving to obtain industrial peace, between both labor and management and between different firms and proprietors, full employment, and, of course, justice for everyone involved in the work. But there is a second task, of even greater importance, also naturally arising from the work itself.

In order to understand what this second task is, it is necessary to recall the reasons why the human race engages in economic activity. Why, even, do we have the capacity to engage in such activity? The answer, as I said above, is that we need to do so in order to obtain the material objects we need to live. And by *live* we certainly mean not merely bodily survival, but life as human beings, in a civilized community, with appropriate family, social, intellectual and spiritual pursuits. If this is true, then economic activity exists for a purpose, and is therefore subordinate to that purpose. Economic activity, then, must be judged by how well it fulfills its purposes, by how well it contributes to and supports the living of a full human life by all, a life that is a fitting preparation for the life to come. Too often, though, economic activity does not fulfill this function well. If an economic system fosters gross inequality, materialistic consumerism, degrades the environment and disrupts family and community life by its feverish pulse, its continual "creative" destruction, then it does not accomplish well that for the sake of which it exists.

But how can we see to it that economic activity adequately fulfills its purpose? The two answers usually proposed, as I said above, are both wrong. The first is that if only economic activity is left alone, or nearly so, then the free market will take care of the problem. Men, by means of their many individual choices, motivated only by a desire to maximize their gains and minimize their losses, will unerringly direct economic activity into serving the common good. But this supposition is entirely wrong. A free market indeed serves human wishes, but whose and of what sort? There is a difference between human needs and human wants, and especially between the wants of the powerful and the rich, and the needs of the community. Free competition does allow those with most power or resources to make choices and act upon them, but what is to guarantee that their choices also promote the common good? As Pope Pius XI wrote, "unrestrained free competition... permits the survival of those only who are the strongest. This often means those who fight most relentlessly, who pay least heed to the dictates of conscience" (Encyclical *Quadragesimo Anno*, no. 107). But the more basic problem with this attempted solution to the economic question is the false notion that "unregulated competition [is] a principle of self-direction more suitable for guiding [economic activity] than any created intellect which might intervene," as Pius XI further noted in the same encyclical (no. 88). In other words, just as in every other human activity, from digging a garden to fighting a war, suitable planning and guidance must be exercised if the proper end is to be obtained, so also in economic affairs. The free market solution, then, is wrong because it misunderstands human nature and the human community, while the second commonly advanced solution, direct intervention by the central government, though more realistic about the need to intervene in the economy, also is mistaken, because of its reliance on centralized planning.

Though both of these approaches are wrong, nevertheless the problem is quite real. How can we insure, to the best of our ability, that all the multifarious economic undertakings of man really work together to promote human life on this earth, the life of man in the family, the community, the Church? Here again, the occupational group is the answer, for the second task of occupational groups is to orient the activity of the industry or profession in question toward the common good, to see to it that the products made or the services provided are useful, well-made or well-performed, fairly priced, and advertised without fraud or exaggeration. According to Pius XI, this second task of the occupational group is the more important. He wrote, " . . . it is easy to conclude that in these associations the common interest of the whole 'group' must predominate: and among these interests the most important is the directing of the activities of the group to the common good" (*Quadragesimo Anno*, no. 85). In other words, an occupational group will not be doing its duty if, although the industry is flourishing, with both employees and employers receiving generous sums, this is being done at the expense of the public, either through shoddy items, unfair prices, the introduction of products which are harmful, useless or debasing to society, or dangerous to the environment.

The twin tasks of occupational groups are therefore, to bring order to the existing unity in an industry or profession so that all can work harmoniously together for prosperity; and secondly, to orient the industry or profession toward genuine service to society. Now how are these noble aims to be attained?

In the case of the first aim, that of bringing internal order to an industry, one can recognize that industrial disorder comes about from strife between labor and management or from strife among different firms. Moreover, in both cases, an end to discord based on one side being crushed not only fails to create a stable solution but as well constitutes an injustice. But a lessening of discord based on submission to a higher rule of justice does have the potential to bring about genuine peace, at least as much as fallen man can hope to have. Such a result in industrial relations requires that all parties recognize the legitimate claims of the others. And by "legitimate claims" I do not mean simply that by a process of give and take and compromise all will get less than they want for the sake of the whole. No, I mean that all sides will recognize an overarching standard by which the validity of their own and of others' demands can be judged and measured.

In regard to wages, for example, if we recognize that all men, simply as men, have the right to live in human dignity, and that normally the only means people have to obtain the necessary sums to do so is by their labor, then we will recognize a worker's right to a wage sufficient to allow for such dignity. Thus a living family wage will not be a concession grudgingly granted as the outcome of tough negotiations, nor as a charitable largess, but as something that is simply the due of the worker, something he naturally should expect and receive. Similarly with a level of profits for the firm adequate for maintenance of the industry: the costs of doing business, rehabilitation and enhancement of physical facilities, replacement of capital, etc. Since these are all necessary they can be granted without feeling that management has somehow triumphed. Likewise with a salary for managers and a return on investment for owners and bondholders that is reasonable, an amount proportionate for the time or money invested in the business. Management and owners do not have the right simply to dispose according to their will of whatever money is not needed for labor, production and other costs, for everything connected with the industry must be judged according to justice and the common good.[32] If we grant that the profits of an industry must be distributed according to reason and justice, rather than power, then there will be considerably less friction between management and labor over these questions. A living wage can be calculated if both parties will give up the practice, a practice which labor learned from management, of trying to gain as much as possible with little thought for justice or the common welfare.

The strife between companies producing the same product likewise contributes to industrial instability. If the struggle between labor and management can be lessened or eliminated by looking to what is just and reasonable, so can that between different firms. Strife between firms largely concerns matters of market share. If the market for a particular item is only so large, then obviously a firm can sell more only by reducing the market share and profits of its competitors. This they all attempt to do in various ways, by pricing, advertising, product design and quality, reducing costs, etc. All this is the cause, however, not only of much industrial instability, frequently resulting in layoffs, plant closings and suchlike, but of deception of the consuming public as well by deceitful advertising and shoddy but appealing products. But if different firms making the same product would regard themselves as cooperating to provide the public with a needed item or service, rather than as competing to gain as large a profit as possible,[33] then some kind of self-regulation naturally

---

32 See Miller, *Forty Years After*, pp. 103–107.
33 Richard Tawney's book, *The Acquisitive Society* (New York:

suggests itself. If firms agree to share the market based on factors such as the public's real need for the product or service, the various firms' capacities to produce, production levels required by each firm to make a reasonable profit, etc., then no one's reasonable interests will be injured, though unbounded acquisitive desires might well be thwarted.

The methods by which an occupational group might reach solutions to such problems could include the following: require all unions and firms in an industry to reach joint collective bargaining decisions, or perhaps extend to the entire industry a model agreement when a certain percentage of the industry has ratified it;[34] require all firms within the industry to participate in negotiating market sharing agreements; frame industry-wide safety standards and enforce them by mixed worker/management committees; negotiate industry-wide contracts with suppliers of raw materials. Of course, all concerned must be fairly represented in reaching these decisions and agreements.

All these things involve the internal structure of an industry, either labor/management relations or relations among different companies. What of the second but more important aim of occupational groups, that of orienting the industry toward the common good?

Harcourt, Brace and World, 1920) contains a chapter, "Industry as a Profession," pp. 91 to 122, which is a very good discussion of the notion of all work as a necessary service to the public, i.e., a profession, and thus rightly subject to the same kinds of restraints and standards of conduct that at least formerly were associated with the professions. See especially pp. 94 to 97.

34 "Within one of Germany's autonomous regions, an identical wage and salary system applies to all companies in a particular branch of industry. Because most companies are members of an employers' association, and are thus bound by the collective wage agreement, the agreement virtually has the weight of a statutory law." Uwe Liebig, "Dialogue Instead of Confrontation," p. 55.

As I said above, the relationship of an industry or profession to service to the public embraces primarily the following topics: the quality of the goods or services provided, and whether they are truly beneficial to society; fairness of prices or fees; truthful advertising; and possible harm to the environment during the production process or during use of the product. What would an occupational group do to in regard to these matters? The medieval guilds, the occupational groups of their day, in order to insure that only quality products were sold to the public, carefully superintended the production of craft or industrial articles. Guild representatives sought to make sure that only raw materials which met guild standards were used, and that the process of production likewise met its criteria. It seems to me that something analogous would need to be done by occupational groups today. In earlier times, in fact, when manufacturing processes were much simpler, the resultant finished product was easier to examine for flaws or shoddy workmanship. Today inferior mechanisms can hide beneath a shiny coat of thin metal, and most consumers are not capable of judging the complex technology of machines. Especially with regard to major purchases, such as washing machines or refrigerators, buyer choice in the market has little influence over manufacturers, for even though the consumer may be disappointed by the product quality, the fact that he is unlikely to buy another such item for many years, considerably detracts from his ability to influence manufacturers' practices by his choices in the marketplace. But even with frequently used items, such as soap or toothpaste, a consumer rarely can accurately gauge the product's worth. Thus it would seem that careful supervision of production by occupational group representatives, with powers to impose fines or other punishments, is necessary to guarantee product quality.

The question of whether or not a particular product or service is truly beneficial to society or merely a means of moneymaking, is more complicated. But since it ultimately involves considerations of the common good, it is a matter in which those charged with care of the temporal common good, the state authorities, must be involved. This is true even though an occupational group's competence and official concerns extend to the industry's relations with the public and others, because such a group's mission is still necessarily specialized and narrow.

The question of fair prices is complex. The medieval guilds frankly and firmly set prices for their members, or they were set by the state or municipal authorities, and in the context of the more static medieval economy this undoubtedly resulted in just prices for consumers. There are many different opinions, however, on how best to accomplish this same aim today. Setting of prices by occupational groups or the state is unquestionably licit, but it is a question of prudence whether or not it is the best contemporary method for achieving justice in pricing. One approach would be merely to publish figures as to production and other costs, plus an indication of a fair profit, thus forcing each producer to adhere to a just price through force of public opinion and buyer choice in the marketplace. Still others have suggested that only very excessive monopoly prices or very low prices that result from low wages and give an unfair competitive edge, or from an unjust situation, as in a large chain competing against a small concern, should be controlled. As a matter of fact, if all the pacts between firms and the industry-wide labor-management agreements that I mentioned above were implemented, firms would naturally tend toward similar and just prices.[35] In

---

35   In regard to just prices, see John F. Cronin, *Catholic Social Principles*, pp. 295–298 and the same author's *Economics and Society* (New York: American Book Company, 1939), pp. 108–111.

any case, although a just price may at times be difficult to calculate, commutative justice demands that a thing be sold for what it is worth and no more.[36] Ordinarily this would be connected with reasonable costs of doing business.

Advertising must be conceived of as more a way of informing the public as to what is available and at what price, than of persuading anyone to buy an item. And if this is so, then several firms could advertise jointly, simply listing what was for sale and at what price. Since advertising is obviously directly accessible to the public, it should be easy to establish a mechanism whereby complaints about misleading advertising could be lodged with the firm in question, with appeals possible to the occupational group, and perhaps after that to a special tribunal conducted by the federation of all occupational groups, or to special or ordinary courts.[37]

In the last area, that of possible harm to the environment, the firm itself would obviously be responsible in the first instance for insuring that its productive processes and finished products were harmless and safe, but again supervision by the

---

Under the National Recovery Administration (1933–1935), the only serious attempt in the United States to establish an orderly industrial arrangement for the common good of the entire economy, each industry set, usually via its so-called code authority, *minimum* prices. This was an attempt to eliminate the practice of ruthless competition — with accompanying substandard wages — by tying prices to cost of production, including adequate wages. See George Terborgh, *Price Control Devices in NRA Codes* (Washington: Brookings Institution, 1934) and Leverett S. Lyon et al., *The National Recovery Administration, an Analysis and Appraisal* (Washington: Brookings Institution, 1935), pp. 578–622. The latter work comments (p. 578), "It would seem hardly necessary to explain that, for all practical purposes, the power to fix a minimum price is in effect the power to fix price."

36 See *Summa Theologiae* II–II q. 77, art. 1.

37 Advertising, with all its misrepresentations and outright lies, now seems a natural part of life to us, but this was not always so. See Fanfani, *Catholicism, Protestantism and Capitalism*, pp. 33 and 79–80.

occupational group would be necessary. In case of disputes, or complaints from the public, recourse would be available to the occupational-group federation, and finally to the state.

A few more things must be said about the organization and working of occupational groups before this section ends. In the first place, a typical occupational group will be organized, first on a local basis, then on a regional basis, then on the national level. (Under proper government supervision, occupational groups might well have some kind of international aspect, being affiliated with like groups in other countries, especially major trading partners.) Matters will be handled at the local level where possible, and at the regional and national when necessary or fitting. Moreover, as I intimated above, at the national level all the various occupational groups will be linked together to coordinate in a cooperative manner the entire national economy, not to impose centralized planning, but to endeavor to make the economy work harmoniously, to avoid depressions and recessions, etc. This inter-occupational organization could well have certain powers to hear appeals from its member groups. It should be noted, though, that on these organizational matters, the structure of the groups might well differ from country to country or even from industry to industry within a country. It is not in the spirit of Catholic teaching to impose any kind of blueprint on these groups — given proper recognition, encouragement and guidance, they will take form and begin to exercise their functions on their own.[38]

---

38 This is the meaning of the often misunderstood or misrepresented passage from John Paul's *Centesimus Annus*, no. 43. "The Church has no models to present; models that are real and truly effective can only arise within the framework of different historical situations, through the efforts of all those who responsibly confront concrete problems in all their social, economic, political and cultural aspects, as these interact with one another."

Occupational groups will also likely take charge of many things that are now the direct concern either of the state or of the individual. For example, occupational groups might own and run trade or technical schools or otherwise provide apprenticeship and training to members or prospective members; they properly would provide insurance to members and their families, and, as I will speak more of below, they might own industrial banks to provide for their own business financing.

Secondly, it must be emphasized that although occupational groups are independent and self-governing bodies, and not organs of the state, they are not voluntary associations, which one is free to join or not. Everyone working or producing in a particular industry or profession would be required to join his occupational group, and the regulations of the occupational group would be backed by the force of law. This is obviously necessary if their work is to have any effect on the economy. Nor is this an infringement on legitimate freedom, for true economic freedom consists in the freedom to make a reasonable and sufficient living by serving some need of oneself or the community. Any economic freedom compatible with a community that values family and social life above moneymaking simply cannot be freedom to amass unlimited amounts of money, especially at the expense of others or of the stability of the community. If one has enough for a reasonable and comfortable human existence, then true freedom does not require the opportunity to acquire more, especially if that acquisition involves hurting others economically or socially, by taking over their markets, driving them out of business, closing factories, relocating workers and breaking up communities and families. It is difficult to see, for example, why the owners of a large and profitable chain of fast food stores, if they already are rich, should have the liberty to continue to expand at the expense of small restaurants and food outlets, whose owners, perhaps, are struggling to survive and to support their own families. G. K. Chesterton's remark, to the effect that the institution of private property no more implies the right to acquire unlimited property than the institution of marriage implies the right to acquire unlimited wives, is appropriate to recall here.[39]

The last thing to be noted about the organization of occupational groups, one which I stated earlier and wish only to underscore here, is that they will contain and represent all involved in a particular industry, workers, managers and owners. Though the occupational groups will insure that all points of view and interests are adequately heard, and though on certain issues separate votes by subgroup might well need to be taken,[40] the occupational group as a whole will represent all regardless of their position on the labor market. Otherwise the group will be a formal expression of class division and conflict, rather than of the organic unity arising from the interconnection of one man's work with that of his fellows. Occupational groups are to aid in binding a community together, not be agents of its division into warring halves.

It will be helpful to quote the summary of the occupational group's functions made by the greatest American theologian of social doctrine, Msgr. John A. Ryan. He wrote,

> The occupational group might be empowered by law to fix wages, interest, dividends, and prices, to determine working conditions, to adjust industrial disputes, and to carry on whatever economic planning was thought feasible. All the groups in the several

---

39 *What's Wrong With the World* (Peru, Ill.: Sherwood Sugden, n.d.), p. 36 (chap. 6).

40 *Quadragesimo Anno*, no. 85.

concerns of an industry could be federated into a national council for the whole industry. There could also be a federation of all the industries of the nation. The occupational groups, whether local or national, would enjoy power and authority over industrial matters coming within their competence. This would be genuine self-government in industry.

Of course, the occupational groups would not be entirely independent of the government. No economic group, whether of capitalists or laborers, or of both in combination, can be trusted with unlimited power to fix their own profits and remuneration. While allowing to the occupational groups the largest measure of reasonable freedom in the management of their own affairs, the State, says Pius XI, should perform the tasks which belong to it and which it alone can effectively accomplish, namely, those of "directing, watching, stimulating, and restraining, as circumstances suggest or necessity demands...."[41]

Moreover, and lastly, though we have seen how occupational groups are to insure the provision of justice, a word must be added about social charity. As Pius XI, again in *Quadragesimo Anno*, said (no. 137),

> Charity cannot take the place of justice unfairly withheld, but, even though a state of things be pictured in which every man receives at last all that is his due, a wide field will nevertheless remain open for charity. For, justice alone, even though most faithfully observed, can remove indeed the cause of social strife, but can never bring about a union of hearts and minds. Yet this union, binding men together, is the main principle of stability in all institutions, no matter how perfect they may

---

41 *Distributive Justice*, pp. 340–41.

seem, which aim at establishing social peace and promoting mutual aid. In its absence, as repeated experience proves, the wisest regulations come to nothing. Then only will it be possible to unite all in harmonious striving for the common good, when all sections of society have the intimate conviction that they are members of a single family and children of the same Heavenly Father....

If some wonder how occupational groups are to accomplish all that is demanded of them, remember that they will accomplish very little without the social charity which must be the soul of this social order. And there is no reason to be unwilling to admit that social charity cannot exist without the working of Almighty God. This last fact, however, clearly shows that the reform of institutions cannot be thought of apart from the reform of morals, and this continues to involve us in considerations of how best to promote and safeguard Catholic faith within a Catholic culture and a Catholic state.

IV

Capitalism no more means the affirmation of an individual, or a family's right to possess land, machinery, housing, clothing, reserves of food and the rest, than fatty degeneration of the heart means the normal function of the heart as the circulator of the blood in a healthy human body. — Hilaire Belloc[42]

In section III of this chapter I discussed the occupational group in detail, but without specific reference to any other changes that would be necessary in order to make an

---

42 *The Crisis of Civilization* (Rockford, Ill.: TAN Books, 1992 printing) p. 139.

economic system conform to the ideal of a Catholic society. Although it is impossible, when speaking on as general a level as I am, to lay down too specific prescriptions, still certain things demand discussion. And the first is the question of capitalism itself.

I remind the reader of the definition of capitalism given above and gathered from *Quadragesimo Anno* no. 100, namely "that economic system in which were provided by different people the capital and labor jointly needed for production."[43] There is no question but that a system based largely on such an arrangement can be in itself just. Nevertheless, I think such a system is unwise and dangerous for the following two reasons: First, because under it some men are mainly suppliers of capital and thus one step removed from the process of production itself, they tend to see the economic system in terms not of production for human needs, but of manipulation of money, stocks, bonds, and other financial instruments for their own profit. In other words, finance comes to be an end in itself, or more precisely, the economic system is conceived of as existing for the sake of making some people rich through financial transactions, rather than for the sake of supplying our necessary material needs. Second, the separation of ownership from labor tends to create a permanent class of non-owning workers, a circumstance often deplored by the popes, and one which exacerbates class feeling and class warfare. This situation in turn produces men alienated from their work and dulled in spirit.[44] If the managers and directors of corporations had

---

43 See note 17 above.
44 Fr. Cahill, who defines capitalism exactly as I do, says of it: "But although the capitalist régime is not essentially vicious, the Church's tendency has always been more in favour of a system in which the dominating portion of the workers are owners or part owners of the capital with which they labour. The Christian social ideal, which emphasizes

to work in coal mines and on assembly lines we would soon see drastic changes in such work. When one contrasts the wonderful cooperative work of the medieval craft guilds, who put on complicated and lavish religious dramas each year, with the modern worker spending his leisure time in front of his television set, we might well ask ourselves if being in charge of one's own work does not have consequences far beyond the workplace itself.[45]

---

so strongly the dignity and privileges of human personality, is more easily realised in a social system which includes the widest extension of ownership." *The Framework of a Christian State*, pp. 137–38.

45   No social or economic arrangements can bring about a Utopia, but even in our fallen world some are better than others. Under capitalism some men are in a sense tools of those who are the owners of capital. Even when the directors and their managers have good reasons for making a decision which is perceived as detrimental to the workers, the workers do not know what the reasons are and have no opportunity of joining in making the decision about what is best for the enterprise. To choose an example that I have heard about myself, in a certain mining enterprise in the U. S., when work is slack, the manager lays off the miners for *four* days at a time, since they cannot obtain unemployment benefits (which the firm is required to contribute to) unless they are laid off for *five* consecutive days. The management apparently claims that the firm cannot afford the extra outlay for unemployment benefits. Is this just? Does the firm need to do this in order to survive? The point is that the workers do not know. Perhaps the management is right and this is the only way the enterprise can continue to exist. And since the mine pays comparatively high wages for that region, people continue to work there. But it would seem that the workers have an interest, if not a right, to participate in such a decision. If the management is indeed correct, the workers might well agree with that decision, if they had access to the facts. They cannot be treated as mere pawns, to be moved about as though they were not rational creatures. As John Paul II wrote in *Laborem Exercens* (no. 15), "the person who works desires *not only* due *remuneration* for his work; he also wishes that, within the production process, provision be made for him to be able to *know* that in his work, even on something that is owned in common, he is working `for himself.'" [emphasis in original] The Pontiff goes on to say that when he is a tool of a bureaucracy — and that would be true whether

But if capitalism — that is, the separation of labor from capital — were eliminated, what would replace it? I think that the replacement truest to the Catholic spirit would doubtless be a society of owner-operators, that is, small businesses, whether stores or workshops or service businesses or farms. Such establishments would need to be very small by today's standards, for the ideal is surely for every worker to have the chance of becoming an owner. Thus each owner-employer could hardly have more than two or three hired workers, who themselves would be, formally or informally, learning the skills of the work in question and hoping eventually to become owners themselves. But for enterprises which needed large workforces and big machines, cooperative ownership by the workers themselves would be the obvious way of avoiding the noxious separation of capital and labor.[46]

Moreover, the widespread ownership of productive property would have consequences beyond the simply economic. For it would still be necessary for these small-owners to be

that bureaucracy were capitalistic, socialistic or even cooperative — the worker feels that he is "a mere production instrument rather than a true subject of work with an initiative of his own." Capitalism, with its separation of ownership from work, does not normally allow a worker to be a "true subject of work."

46   While it is true that papal teaching has never condemned capitalism as defined here as in itself unjust, still in their social encyclicals the popes have repeatedly urged widespread property ownership as a partial remedy for the "wage slavery" of the working class. See, for example, *Rerum Novarum*, nos. 4, 10, 26, 35; *Quadragesimo Anno*, nos. 59–62, 65; *Mater et Magistra*, nos. 85–89, 91–93, 111–115; *Laborem Exercens*, no. 14.

Fanfani's comment is worth noting, "But if the Catholic Church often finds nothing to which to take exception in the private instruments of capitalism, she finds much to blame in the end to which they are directed and the manner in which they are organized." *Catholicism, Protestantism and Capitalism*, p. 141.

See Appendix I for a discussion of two varying Catholic approaches to the question of ownership and the wage system.

organized into their occupational groups in order to avoid economic strife over market share and to prevent some owners from enlarging their establishments at the expense of their fellow producers. In fact, unless the existence of the natural bond of the occupational group is made manifest, men will tend to view their fellow producers as competitors, instead of as what they are, namely, brothers in providing for the needs of their fellow men. And, as in the Middle Ages, such Catholic occupational groups can be expected to become main agents in the promotion of social charity, establishing insurance funds for their members and their widows and orphans. The medieval occupational groups — the guilds — celebrated the festivals of the patron saints of their trades, employed chaplains to say Mass for their dead, and otherwise contributed to the intricate interlocking religious and social order that characterized medieval Europe. In addition, as established cooperative corporations with their own membership and treasury, occupational groups could be an important counterweight to any excesses on the part of the government. One of the ways in which medieval society provided checks on the abuse of power by the monarch and his court was by establishing other centers of power and wealth, with their own traditional rights and privileges. If the king were minded to overthrow the traditional rights of his subjects, he might have to reckon with an established and well-organized opposition, very jealous of its immemorial rights and with enough know-how and wealth to stand up for them. Occupational groups are thus an important aspect of a society which is to contain many other kinds of intermediate bodies — towns, well-endowed universities, cooperatives of many kinds — and whose citizens will be members of many subsidiary parts of the whole social body, what Pius XI called "the highly developed social life which once flourished in a variety of prosperous and interdependent institutions...."[47] In fact, a Catholic society will necessarily be marked by the existence of many such groups, each of which fulfills some important social or economic role and each of which directly or indirectly supports all the others. Men will see themselves as members of various corporate bodies and not as lone individuals. The social role of the occupational groups and of the other cooperatives will be at least as important as their economic, for they are the chief means of both overcoming individualism and of uniting men into the rich tapestry of a solid social life.

The chief remaining subjects which it is necessary to discuss have to do with the role of money. Logically speaking, money is secondary in the economic process, for this process exists to provide us with needed material goods and services. But we cannot eat money nor wear it nor make music with it. Yet in recent times, money, and other surrogates for real wealth, such as shares of stock, have assumed a role as if they were what the economy was all about. As a result there are several points about money which must be examined, the first of which is the question of usury.

Usury is a complex topic and the term itself is generally understood today differently from its classic usage in moral theology. Let us begin by quoting from the most complete papal treatment of the subject, the encyclical *Vix Pervenit* (1745) of Pope Benedict XIV.

---

47 *Quadragesimo Anno*, no. 78. Compare also John Paul II, "According to *Rerum Novarum* and the whole social doctrine of the Church, the social nature of man is not completely fulfilled in the State, but is realized in various intermediary groups, beginning with the family and including economic, social, political and cultural groups which stem from human nature itself and have their own autonomy, always with a view to the common good." *Centesimus Annus*, no. 13.

> The nature of the sin called usury has its proper
> place and origin in a loan contract. This financial
> contract between consenting parties demands, by
> its very nature, that one return to another only
> as much as he has received. The sin rests on the
> fact that sometimes the creditor desires more than
> he has given. Therefore he contends some gain is
> owned him beyond that which he loaned, but any
> gain which exceeds the amount he gave is illicit
> and usurious.

One cannot condone the sin of usury by arguing that the
gain is not great or excessive, but rather moderate or small;
neither can it be condoned by arguing that the borrower
is rich; nor even by arguing that the money borrowed is
not left idle, but is spent usefully, either to increase one's
fortune . . . or to engage in business transactions. The law
governing loans consists necessarily in the equality of what
is given and returned; once the equality has been established,
whoever demands more than that violates the terms of the
loan. . . .

By these remarks, however, We do not deny that at times
together with the loan contract certain other titles — which
are not at all intrinsic to the contract — may run parallel with
it. From these other titles, entirely just and legitimate reasons
arise to demand something over and above the amount due
on the contract.

For most contemporaries this sounds odd and perhaps
even contrary to reason, for does not a lender deprive himself
of present money, and since he will receive the principal back
only later, is it not simply just that he receive something over
and above the principal to compensate him for the temporary
loss? The short answer to this is No, for unless the creditor
can point to some loss he will incur because he made the

loan, or to some lost opportunity for legitimate gain, the mere fact of having made a loan does not give him the right to receive interest payments.

The legal and theological starting point which theologians and canonists for centuries employed when considering usury was the Roman law contract known as *mutuum*. This type of contract governed the loan of something which was necessarily consumed in its use, and therefore the identical object could not be returned to the lender, only something of the same kind and amount.

> The subject-matter of the *mutuum* must consist of things that can be measured, weighed, or numbered, such as wine, corn, or money; that is, things which being consumed can be restored *in genere*.... From the nature of this contract the obligation is imposed upon the borrower to restore to the lender, not the identical thing loaned, but its equivalent — that is, another thing of the same kind, quality, and value....

With regard to the responsibility for loss, since from the peculiar character of the contract the right of consumption passes to the borrower, the latter is looked upon as the practical owner of the thing loaned, and he therefore holds it entirely at his own risk....[48]

The chief characteristic of the *mutuum* contract that differentiates it from any other type of loan is that the actual good borrowed is not returned but consumed or used up by the borrower. This is in contrast to the loan or rent of something which will be physically returned, such as a house or a car. Hence any claim for compensation beyond the face value

---

48   William C. Morey, *Outlines of Roman Law.* (New York: G. P. Putman's, 2d ed., 1914), 355–56.

of the loan based on wear and tear is not a factor in evaluating compensation for the lender in a contract of *mutuum*.[49]

Let us illustrate the classic argument against usury with an example taken not from money, but from food and drink. Suppose we have a small businessman who owns a catering service, catering food and drink, and let us suppose further that any supplies which accompany the food and drink are disposable, plastic forks, paper napkins, etc., so that there is nothing which he provides to his customers which can be reused and therefore is subject to wear and tear. Now what may he licitly charge his customers for? For the replacement cost of the food and drink and the other disposable supplies. In addition, he may charge each customer for a share of the overhead of his business, such as rent, utilities, his delivery van, wages for any employees, and for a salary for himself, which may be defined as a "return for his labor of organization and direction, and for the risk that he underwent."[50] But as regards the food and other consumptibles which he provides, it is hard to see how he can charge a customer for more than the amount purchased. If he furnishes 100 bottles of wine, the caterer may charge what it will cost him to replace a similar kind and amount of wine. Anything additional which he charges a customer must come from one of the other titles I just mentioned, costs incident to the running of his business and wages for his employees and for himself.

The application of this to money loans can easily be seen. Instead of food and wine, if the matter of the *mutuum* is money, again it is hard to see how a debtor can be expected to repay more than he was loaned in the first place, although, as

---

49   St. Thomas Aquinas discusses usury in the context of a *mutuum* contract in the *Summa Theologiae* II–II, q. 78. See also *De Malo*, q. 13, a. 4.

50   John A. Ryan, *Distributive Justice*, p. 176.

in the case of our caterer, he may justly be expected to pay a fair share of incidental costs. In the Middle Ages there existed institutions called *montes pietatis*, lending institutions created to provide an alternative to usurers, sponsored by local governments or the Church. The *montes* were non-profit institutions, but they charged interest to cover their expenses, including salaries of their staff.

Of course our caterer receives immediate or nearly immediate payment for his expenditure on food and other consumptibles. A loan of money, however, is generally paid back after a period of time, or gradually during such a period. Is not the lender entitled to some compensation on account of this delay? No, for " . . . the mere time differential by itself does not cause a difference in value. There must be added the possibility of earning a profit in the intervening time period."[51] That is the meaning of the words of Pope Benedict XIV, that

> We do not deny that at times together with the loan contract certain other titles — which are not at all intrinsic to the contract — may run parallel with it. From these other titles, entirely just and legitimate reasons arise to demand something over and above the amount due on the contract.

Historically the chief parallel titles were *lucrum cessans* and *damnum emergens*. The former is the loss of opportunity for gain — say an opportunity of becoming a partner in a business venture — which someone might forgo by making a loan, and the latter is some actual damage which he might suffer by not having the funds available which he had loaned, for

---

51   Heinrich Pesch, *Lehrbuch der Nationalökonomie/Teaching Guide to Economics*, translated by Rupert J. Ederer (Lewiston: Edwin Mellen, c. 2003), vol. 5, book, 2, p. 200.

example, not having sufficient cash on hand to pay his taxes and thereby incurring a penalty. But it is crucial to recognize that the mere fact of making a loan does not equate to the right to repayment of more than the principal, for there is nothing in the loan transaction itself that entitles him to any interest payment.[52]

The praxis of the Church, beginning at least in the first half of the 19th century, was to presume that some justifying title to interest probably exists in most cases in the context of a complex modern finance economy. This point of view was embodied in the (now abrogated) 1917 Code of Canon Law which restated the doctrine of *Vix Pervenit* while allowing in practice for the taking of interest under other titles.[53] The Church is assuming that parallel titles which justify interest exist in the vast majority of cases, and that even if in some cases they do not, it is better for the sake of consciences to ignore that fact than to attempt the complex task of disentangling the various elements of the contract.

Now although we may admit that much modern interest taking might not be usury — it may be justified by one of the

---

52 Another way of looking at this example which yields the same conclusion is to regard a *mutuum* of money as a *sale*. As in the case of the caterer who provides 100 bottles of wine and receives as part of his total payment the price of the 100 bottles, no more and no less, if we look at money loaned as a sale of money we see that the price of $100 is obviously $100. Any other just charges come from the same titles as the caterer had, overhead expenses, wages, etc. For the product provided one can charge only what it is worth, which in the case of money is its face value.

53 Canon 1543 of the 1917 Code of Canon Law ran, "If a fungible thing is given to someone in such a way that it becomes his and later is to be returned only in the same kind, no gain can be received by reason of the contract itself; but in the payment of a fungible thing, it is not in itself illicit to contract for the gain allowed by law, unless it is clear that this is excessive, or even for a greater gain, if a just and adequate title be present." There is no comparable canon in the 1983 Code.

legitimate titles that are not intrinsic to a loan contract — still one may question whether a system based on routine interest taking is all for the best. If our economy were dedicated more directly toward production for fulfilling human needs and the economic stability that promotes social stability, then the need for the complex financial instruments used by capitalists in their various transactions would be largely obviated and probably also the occasion for legitimate interest. Muslims, moreover, even in the context of twentieth-century capitalism, have maintained and actually expanded a banking system which is based upon the principle of no interest.[54] One can regret that Catholics did not oppose more stalwartly the introduction of economic practices that are dependent on routine interest taking for their smooth operation.

One additional practice involving money that many have questioned is the role of the banking system as creators of money. A number of twentieth-century writers, including professional economists,[55] have seriously called into question

---

54   On Islamic banking, see Zubair Iqbal and Abbas Mirakhor, *Islamic Banking* (Washington: International Monetary Fund, 1987), occasional paper no. 49. Most Muslim countries have at least some non-interest banking, and some make use of this solely. Iran and Pakistan have initiated total non-interest banking. See also, Rodney Wilson, ed., *Islamic Financial Markets* (London: Routledge, 1990). Pp. 172–195 have an interesting account of how the government gradually introduced this type of banking in Pakistan.

Also Mansoor Hassan Khan, "Designing an Islamic Model for Project Finance," *International Financial Law Review*, vol. 16, no. 6, June 1997, pp. 13–16. The author states, "For Muslims around the world, Islamic banking holds more than a merely commercial significance because it relates to the fulfilment of the religious obligation to live all spheres of one's life according [to] the tenets of Islam." (p. 13)

55   See, for example, Irving Fisher, *100% Money* (New York: Adelphi, 1935); Milton Friedman, *A Program for Monetary Stability* (New York: Fordham University, 1960); and Rupert J. Ederer, *The Evolution of Money* (Washington: Public Affairs Press, 1964).

the wisdom or justice of our present arrangements. Consider this account from an elementary economics text of how money is created:

> An individual banker might say that his bank cannot create or destroy money. This is true insofar as an individual bank is concerned. But it is not true of our commercial banking system as a whole. Most of the monetary supply is created by the banking system and is withdrawn from the economy when it is not needed.

The ability of the commercial banking system to create money is based on the *fractional reserve* banking method. The basic business of a commercial bank is to accept deposits, most of which are in turn loaned to other customers at interest. The bank makes most of its income from this interest. It can loan money deposited by some of its customers because it knows from long experience that all its depositors are not likely to want to withdraw all their funds at the same time. In other words, it is only necessary that a bank keep a fractional amount of its deposits on reserve in the form of cash to meet its daily needs.

Let us assume that banks feel that they must keep, or that they are legally required to keep, 20 per cent of all their deposits on hand as a reserve. Then, let us trace what may happen if you deposit $1,000 in a bank. This deposit increases the bank's cash on hand by $1,000. Of this amount, it must keep $200 in reserve, but it can loan $800 to someone else. Assume that the person borrowing the $800 now deposits all of this in a second bank. That bank's deposits increase by $800, of which it can loan $640. If this borrowed $640 is in turn deposited in a third bank, that bank can loan $512. And so it can go, throughout the banking system. All of this may be done by checks; no currency or coins need be involved.

Note, however, that you still have a deposit of $1,000 in your bank. Also, the three borrowers have deposits in other banks in the amounts of $800, $640, and $512, respectively. Each of you can write checks against your deposits. Your original $1,000 has now been expanded to $2,952 in actual buying power — or $1,952 dollars in new deposit money has been created.[56]

What is wrong with the situation here described? In regard to the question of bank-created money, a concept that I think must seem strange to most people when they first become aware of it, two points may be raised. First, since as the text states, a bank "makes most of its income" from the money it loans out at interest, and further, that over half of this money is money the banking system itself creates, out of nothing as it were, is it just for banks to receive interest on money they have created out of nothing? Secondly, is this formidable power over the entire economic system, what Pius XI in *Quadragesimo Anno* called "the life-blood to the entire economic body," (no. 106), rightly exercised by private individuals, that is, privately owned commercial banks, working for their own private profit?

It has seemed to many Catholic economists and students of this problem that the creation of most of our money supply by banks is fundamentally wrong.[57] The alternative generally proposed is for the government to issue all money,

---

56 Roy J. Sampson and Thomas W. Calmus, *Economics: Concepts, Applications, Analysis* (Boston: Houghton Mifflin, c. 1974), pp. 75–76.
57 See Rupert Ederer, "Is Usury Still a Problem?" *Homiletic & Pastoral Review,* August-September 1984, pp. 18–20, and the references he gives there. Moreover, he links money creation by banks with the usury problem. Some other Catholic writers who have espoused the same position on bank created money are Fr. Denis Fahey in *Money Manipulation and Social Order* (Hawthorne, Calif.: Omni Publications, 1986) and Fr. F. H. Drinkwater in *Seven Addresses on Social Justice* (London: Burns, Oates & Washbourne, 1937).

with the money supply keeping pace with the growth of economic activity in the country, and money thus serving its purpose of aiding productive economic activity. The technicalities of this easily bewilder many nonspecialists, yet if one points out that money is not really wealth — money cannot be eaten or drunk or worn — and that, for example, were all coins and currency, as well as other surrogates such as stock certificates, to suddenly vanish, no real wealth would disappear from the country, one sometimes seems able to get people's attention. From this one is led to suspect that manipulations of money and other pieces of paper played a great part in bringing about such calamities as the Great Depression of 1929. In fact, during this period real wealth, for example, milk and farm animals, was actually destroyed, while people starved.[58]

There is another matter regarding banks that is worth discussing. If economic activity exists for the sake of human life, and further, if finance exists for the sake of aiding economic activity, then obviously finance and financial institutions are twice removed from what should be the primary concerns of mankind. One possible way of formalizing this subsidiary role of finance would be for occupational groups, or perhaps federations of occupational groups, to own their own banks in order to provide necessary financing to member businesses. If this were the case, and if the managers of these financial institutions were employees of the occupational groups, it is probable that it would be much easier to keep finance within its proper bounds, that of service to true productive economic activity. Such banks would be for business and industrial purposes only, while consumer credit needs could be served by parallel cooperative banks for the

58 Herbert Feis, *1933: Characters in Crisis* (Boston: Little, Brown, 1966), pp. 10–11.

individual members of the occupational groups, or perhaps by cooperative banks (credit unions as they are known in the English-speaking world today) formed directly by the inhabitants of a town, a parish, a religious sodality, etc.

After this long and sometimes technical discussion of economic matters it seems fitting to highlight briefly those features of the economy which would necessarily characterize a Catholic state. And first, for any laws to be properly framed, let alone observed and enforced, the principle must be grasped and accepted that economic activity is to be judged on how well it serves the common good of society. Society must not be twisted and deformed to serve the spurious application of economic laws or questionable principles of morality, such as exaggerated notions of property rights or false ideas of economic freedom. Moreover, the spirit that encourages the amassing of large fortunes likewise must die. With this change of attitude, then, the formal establishment of occupational groups is surely the first thing to be done, and if done correctly, much of the rest will follow of its own accord, or rather, will follow from the logic of an economy devoted to service, not limitless profit. Other laws must eventually bring about the reform of money and banking. But all this will be for nothing if we do not thoroughly understand and unreservedly acknowledge the Christian, and indeed human, view of economic activity, which sees material things, and such surrogates as money, for what they are, and sees what human life in society is intended by God to be. Only then will all the principles, institutions and rules make sense and be used and administered for the glory of God and the true welfare of mankind, as much as our fallen state permits.

4

Censorship

THE QUESTION OF CENSORSHIP IN a Catholic state has two parts. The first part is the necessity of establishing the legitimacy of censorship; the second must be a discussion of prudential matters, e.g., granted that censorship is legitimate, is it wise to do it in these particular circumstances, how should it be done, to what extent, and so on.

In regard to the first part of the question, whether censorship is legitimate, the argument is simple. If someone has no right to harm his fellow by shooting him or giving him poison, can he have the right to harm him by poisoning his mind or his morals? Similarly, if the community can protect itself from menaces to its physical health, e.g., if someone were to try to poison its water supply, can it not also protect itself against danger and harm to its intellectual and moral health? Moreover, protection of the community against intellectual error is often simply a protection against subsequent physical evil, as, for instance, to ban a book that advocated theft would help protect citizens against actual loss of their property.

Now all this of course presupposes that we can identify intellectual error and moral evil and make an informed prudential judgment about potential dangers, but there should be no hesitation about this for an orthodox Catholic. For surely if the Catholic faith is true, then those things which are contrary to the true Faith and to sound morals, which latter are in fact also contrary to our human nature, cannot be helpful to an individual or to society as a whole. And likewise, their advocacy in print and otherwise cannot be helpful.[1] For if the actual practice of these evils tends to undermine society, will not their advocacy do this also? To take an example of an evil that even very few outside the Faith will dispute: if it is wrong to murder, then could it be morally licit to advocate murder? And should the civil law be helpless to restrain speech which promotes such an evil, on the sophistry that only the deed is evil, not the speech? Anyone who understands what speech or writing is, will realize that its persuasive power can be such that often one speaker or writer is truly the author of more acts than any single doer. And it seems disingenuous and hypocritical to argue that, though we can restrain or punish for an act, we are helpless to do so for one who incites to the act.[2]

---

1 Everything here presupposes, of course, the discussion in chapter two about the state's right to regulate the exercise of non-Catholic public religious activity and the corresponding right to private religious freedom. Thus non-Catholic minorities should have the right of printing or importing books and other material they need for their religious services and education, as long as these are not contrary to the natural law. But such production or importation should be done by special channels so as not to get into general circulation and become a danger to the intellectual health of the nation.

2 Ordinary laws in a liberal democracy may be able to punish someone for *direct* incitement to murder, e.g., if one were to write or say that so and so should be killed. But what of *indirect* incitement? For example, some writers have argued that children up to a certain age, ranging from a few days to seven years, should not be considered persons, and that either their parents or the state should be permitted to kill them. Is not this an incitement to murder those children, at least by changing the law so that their murder will be legal? I see no reason why such speech or writing should not be suppressed by the state. Since instances of infanticide actually take place, one can see that the debate is far from being merely hypothetical. And the same thing may be said for arguments or propaganda on behalf of euthanasia. It is obvious that writings advocating abortion or discussing it in a sympathetic light helped pave the way for its legalization.

When censorship is discussed in the United States, favorable reference is often made to Justice Oliver Wendell Holmes, Jr.'s opinion in the Supreme Court case of Schenck v. United States (249 U. S. 47, March 3, 1919), a case arising from the First World War dealing with literature which urged resistance to the draft. But it is instructive to read from what Holmes actually wrote.

> The most stringent protection of free speech would not protect a man in falsely shouting fire in a theatre and causing a panic. It does not even protect a man from an injunction against uttering words that may have all the effect of force. The question in every case is whether the words used are used in such circumstances and are of such a nature as to create a clear and present danger that they will bring about the substantive evils that Congress has a right to prevent. It is a question of proximity and degree. When a nation is at war many things that might be said in time of peace are such a hindrance to its effort that their utterance will not be endured so long as men fight and that no Court could regard them as protected by any constitutional right. It seems to be admitted that if an actual obstruction of the recruiting service were proved, liability for words that produced that effect might be enforced. (*id*. at 52)

I am not maintaining that Justice Holmes's statement agrees entirely with my thesis here; however, I simply point out that the difference between what he states and what I am arguing for is one of degree and prudential judgment. For, as he says, if a connection between words and "substantive evils" is clear and proximate, then the words themselves may be prohibited. Our disagreement is only in the prudential judgment of the amount of "proximity and degree" that is required before some speech or writing may be banned. Holmes apparently thinks that the connection must be immediate and specific, while it seems to me evident that the general advocacy of evils can and does poison individuals and entire societies, and that the connection between advocating evil, or portraying it in an attractive light, and the actual evil acts, need not be specific before the authorities may reasonably take steps to protect the community. If someone is seen pouring poison into the drinking water must we wait until someone actually dies from drinking it before we take any action to restrain or punish? Or must we even wait until we have proven beyond a reasonable doubt that the death resulted from the very dose of poison which the suspect put into the water?

Now all this should be obvious to any clear-thinking Catholic. Indeed, the encyclicals of Leo XIII that deal with what might be called questions of political philosophy, especially *Diuturnum*, *Immortale Dei* and *Libertas Praestantissimum*, clearly teach this doctrine. Consider the following passage from *Libertas*, no. 23.

> Men have a right freely and prudently to propagate throughout the State what things soever are true and honorable, so that as many as possible may possess them; but lying opinions, than which no mental plague is greater, and vices which corrupt the heart and moral life, should be diligently repressed by public authority, lest they insidiously work the ruin of the State. The excesses of an unbridled intellect, which unfailingly end in the oppression of the untutored multitude, are no less rightly controlled by the authority of the law than are the injuries inflicted by violence upon the weak. And this all the more surely, because by far the greater

part of the community is either absolutely unable, or able only with great difficulty, to escape from illusions and deceitful subtleties, especially such as flatter the passions. If unbridled license of speech and of writing be granted to all, nothing will remain sacred and inviolate; even the highest and truest mandates of nature, justly held to be the common and noblest heritage of the human race, will not be spared. Thus, truth being gradually obscured by darkness, pernicious and manifold error, as too often happens, will easily prevail.

I know that for very many people the mere word "censor" provokes such a negative emotional reaction that a calm consideration of the merits and procedures of state censorship seems intolerable. But I would simply urge those readers to consider the matter in the light of the remarks on liberty and community in the introductory chapter, and of Pope Leo XIII's teaching on this subject quoted here. It seems to me clear that if we can ever know right from wrong, then censorship is clearly sometimes both a right and a duty, if we conceive that society ought to protect itself and its weakest members. Of course no system of censorship will be perfect, but our minds must not be fixed on instances of stupid censorship attempts, nor can we condemn the practice in general, any more than we would condemn surgery because of some individual surgeon's mistakes or wrongdoing. As long as man is infected with the weakness resulting from Adam's sin, that is, until the end of the world, we will be susceptible to error and thus will need to safeguard the good of society in its intellectual and moral health.

I might point out, too, that censorship is actually a protection chiefly for the poorest and weakest members of a society. It is primarily the poor who have been injured by the centuries-long liberal revolt against Christian truth and morals, first against the Church's economic and social teaching, and latterly against the very concept of the family and the person. It is the poor who have seen their traditional villages and families ravaged, the minds of their sons and daughters corrupted, their stable world undone. Censorship on behalf of the truth is a service of social justice for the poor and the working class. It is one important task which the Catholic state must undertake, and without it all the other safeguards for the health of society will exist on very shaky foundations.

Would censorship, even if it might prevent some actual evils from taking place, produce a stunted, immature and fearful society? This viewpoint underlies the famous words of John Milton, in his essay of 1644 against censorship, the *Areopagitica*.

> He that can apprehend and consider vice with all her baits and seeming pleasures, and yet abstain, and yet distinguish, and yet prefer that which is truly better, he is the true warfaring Christian. I cannot praise a fugitive and cloistered virtue, unexercised and unbreathed, that never sallies out and sees her adversary, but slinks out of the race where that immortal garland is to be run for, not without dust and heat. Assuredly we bring not innocence into the world, we bring impurity much rather: that which purifies us is trial, and trial is by what is contrary.[3]

But I think that most of us find more than sufficient material in the world that acquaints us with "vice with all her baits and seeming pleasures," so that we hardly need this acquaintance to be artificially strengthened. Moreover, good literature can do much in a vicarious way to promote virtue

---

3   In *Complete Poems and Major Prose* (Indianapolis: Bobbs-Merrill, c. 1957), p. 728.

and show evil in its true colors. This need not be done in a pietistic or simplistic manner, but in fact has always been part of the task of the arts.

It remains to briefly consider in a general way questions of the kinds, limits and means of censorship the Catholic state will employ in safeguarding its citizens. In fact most of them cannot be decided apart from local circumstances and actual attempts to construct and apply censorship laws. But in so far as one can speak generally, I will try to describe how censorship might in practice work.

The first question, of course, is what sorts of things will the Catholic state censor. Naturally today one immediately thinks of pornography and things inciting to unchastity and violence, but there are more fundamental things than this, and pornography will be dealt with in its turn. For first of all, it is intellectual matters that must be treated of. Ultimately ideas govern the conduct of both individuals and civilizations, and the most abstruse writings of metaphysicians will eventually be the most important influence on everyday life.[4] Naturally there are other factors at work also, but by far the most important is the character of the ruling ideas that are accepted, even if only half-consciously, by a culture and especially by its elites.

---

4   Compare this statement from Leo XIII's encyclical *Aeterni Patris.* "Whoever turns his attention to the bitter strifes of these days and seeks a reason for the troubles that vex public and private life must come to the conclusion that a fruitful cause of the evils which now afflict, as well as those which threaten, us lies in this: that false conclusions concerning divine and human things, which originated in the schools of philosophy, have now crept into all the orders of the State, and have been accepted by the common consent of the masses. For, since it is in the very nature of man to follow the guide of reason in his actions, if his intellect sins at all his will soon follows; and thus it happens that false opinions, whose seat is in the understanding, influence human actions and pervert them." no. 2.

What then will a Catholic state do? Stated briefly, it will prohibit advocacy and free discussion of ideas which are erroneous and which will cause grave harm to individuals or tend to undermine the state and society, insofar as state and society are founded on truth. That is, no one would be allowed to argue on behalf of erroneous philosophical or theological systems nor would free discussion of them be allowed in books or periodicals intended for general circulation. Of course, in universities and learned books and periodicals there would have to be considerable freedom of discussion. Thus authors who advocate error would need to be read and discussed, their ideas commented on, their influence traced, etc. Otherwise no real intellectual life is possible. But this discussion could never extend to actual *advocacy* of these erroneous ideas.

There is no doubt that it would sometimes be difficult to know when someone had crossed the sometimes fine line from discussion to advocacy, from expounding an erroneous idea to promoting it. It is also very clear that one can imagine enormous abuses on the part of the censors, the stifling of insights, as well as corrupting and hypocritical efforts to evade stupid and heavy-handed censorship, much as the *philosophes* of 18th century France evaded the official censorship of the decaying monarchy. The only remedy for this is that the intellectuals and scholars of a Catholic state be really Catholic. Indeed, if they are not, then the state and culture will not endure and all the efforts set forth in this book are in vain. Unless those who think and write and study and learn are really committed to Catholic truth, and thus will work in good faith and realize that mistakes will occur, both on the part of writers and of officials, can there be any hope for a Catholic state. If there cannot exist a reasonable modus vivendi between scholars and writers on the one hand, and censors on the other, then a Catholic state, and indeed a Catholic culture, is impossible. But if censorship can be conducted in an intelligent and reasonable manner, then, despite the inevitable errors that will occur, a body of Catholic intellectuals and artists will be able to exist and flourish under this type of arrangement. We should remember also that the rich intellectual and artistic life of European culture and probably all other cultures of the world was conducted under some form of legal censorship until relatively recently, historically speaking, and proved no barrier to the flourishing of numerous philosophers, historians and artists. And, of course, there is no reason why censors must be narrow-minded bureaucrats, haters of art and of everything new. The ideal censor is someone of liberal education, wide reading, and the ability to reason from first principles. As a matter of fact, any board of censors should contain men from a mixture of backgrounds, writers, artists, lawyers, theologians, philosophers. Among intellectuals truly convinced of the truth of the Catholic faith, such censors would not, at least in principle, be viewed as enemies or fools, but as doing a necessary and honorable task, one that, like all the rest of what is done by the children of Adam, will be done imperfectly. But, like the work of the police or of surgeons, we do not eliminate the function because of those imperfections. Instead we attempt to do the work better.

I said above that in universities and among the learned great freedom of discussion must be allowed. But it would still be necessary to erect safeguards to prevent, as far as possible, the corruption of those exposed to error, especially of university students. The best of these safeguards, though, is surely the clear presentation of the truth and a convincing refutation of the error. Now certainly whenever human beings are involved there is the possibility that something will eventually go awry. So despite any safeguards we may erect, it is possible that reading of books advocating falsehood in universities and among the learned will lead some astray. However, the certain harm that would result were the entire learned class shielded from direct contact with reading such works, works which constitute a necessary part of one's liberal education and of scholarly inquiry, is both more sure and greater than any harm that the reading of these works might bring about. Therefore the risks must be taken and individual cases dealt with as well as possible.

I might add too that when one is thinking of the undergraduate students of the universities, one need not imagine a situation such as obtains in the United States today, where very many study at universities who have no intellectual vocation nor intention to pursue a learned career. Though I think that in a Catholic society education, including advanced degrees, should be absolutely free to all who are capable of mastering the material, still I think that the ideal is for a smaller number of people to receive a higher education than is the case in the U. S. today. Thus those who were exposed to error in their studies would be a smaller percentage of the population, and a more intellectual one, than those who undertake higher education in the contemporary United States.

I imagine a system in which those who by education or position are undertaking serious studies would have a more or less lifetime permission to use any books they needed and subscribe to any journals.[5] Some, such as university teachers, would have this privilege as a matter of course. As for others, perhaps all university graduates could apply for permission,

---

5 Obviously this would not apply to pornography, and there would also be a need for procedures to revoke someone's permission if repeated abuses occurred.

which would be readily granted, and lists kept of those who were allowed this free access. Others could also apply, but would have to prove their fitness and show some good reason for gaining such access. But the officials charged with overseeing such a list should administer the law in the most liberal fashion consonant with the intellectual safety of the society. Their mission is to safeguard intellectual life, not suppress or harass it.

In addition to restricting works whose ideas are erroneous, a Catholic state would need to watch over works of the imagination, that is over novels, poetry, plays, films and the visual arts. Here the danger is different from the case of intellectual argumentation. Literature and the arts usually do not directly and by a series of propositions inculcate particular philosophies. Yet they can very effectively promote a point of view and a kind of behavior, and these can be wrong and harmful to the community.[6] Moreover, even in an artistic or literary creation which basically supports a sound way of life, incidental aspects of the work may be harmful by offending, for example, against standards of chastity or modesty. So again, in these areas the state authorities must be prudently active. Here would be included the question of censorship of pornography.

In cases of censorship of works of the imagination, it would be necessary for the censors to proceed with even greater care than in dealing with intellectual works, since often the meaning of the work, and its likely effect, would

---

6   A valuable but little-known work that discusses the manner in which literature inculcates and advocates ideas and behavior is Austin J. App's *The True Concept of Literature* (San Antonio: Mission Press, 1948). This work would also be a helpful corrective to the simplistic notion that censors should be concerned only or chiefly with exactly how much of the human body is uncovered in a film or how many times certain words are used.

be less clear. But since the power of imaginative literature over the tone and outlook of entire societies is so strong, it is a task that a Catholic state cannot neglect, however difficult it may be to perform.

Clearly it would be impossible to say much more about how such a system of censorship might work in practice, for this is a prudential question that will vary from place to place. It might well involve prepublication approval for certain works or performances, while in other cases, possibly for periodicals, the state can permit publication without previous approval if the editors are trustworthy and understand the law on the matter. And the authorities will have the right to seize material which has been produced or imported illegally, or which is in the wrong hands, as in the case of books which are proper for the learned but not for mass circulation. And since one of the aims of a Catholic state is to have decisions made on the low-est proper level — the principle of subsidiarity — a good deal of the oversight of books and periodicals among the learned might be done by the proper occupational groups and univer-sity faculties themselves. Much of the details would depend on the character of a society, whether there is a strong body which objects to the official goals and policies of the state, or whether the society is basically united around the Faith. And since no public officials can be infallible, there must be provision for appeal and for reconsideration of banned or seized material. But one hopes that writers and artists will be mature enough to understand that there will sometimes be mistakes on the part of the censorship authorities, and that these are no more intolerable than other governmental errors of judgment. One or a few errors will not kill culture or dry up the springs of creativity.

It is also true that even the type of literary or artistic content which is prohibited, and what might be called the degree or the depth of censorship, will vary from culture to culture, depending on factors such as the unity of the people, their Catholic sense, their intellectual and cultural maturity and the proximity of noxious cultural influences from neighboring countries. For example, the relative freedom which medieval writers and visual artists had in treating of sexual matters and the human body might not be appropriate in less intellectually mature cultures, such as those of the twenty-first-century West, but given time and a Catholic environment, rules might be gradually made less restrictive.[7]

---

7 See App, *The True Concept of Literature*, pp. 17–29, for a discussion of the presentation of "sin and temptation in literature." App deals with how a culture's maturity and level of virtue must be taken into account when there is question of what can be portrayed in books or on the stage.

5
Family Law and Other Legal Matters

SOME OF THE MOST STRIKING MAT-
ters with which the state must deal have already been
discussed, matters such as religious liberty, the economy, and censorship. But several very important things still
remain, and among the most important are matters relating
to the family. And in treating of the family other matters will
also be discussed, those which find their proper place as they
relate to the family, for in understanding the centrality of the
family and the proper function of the laws as defending and
favoring the family, we may see the relationship of the law
to other matters, for example, sexuality as a whole, welfare,
and education.

Today we are apt to regard the family as simply one institution among many in society, or as having a purely personal
and subjective significance. Fr. Cahill's words, therefore, are
worth repeating:

> Although the individual is the fundamental unit
> in the State, as in all human associations, it is not
> of individuals as such that the State is immediately
> composed. Between the individual and the State
> the family comes in as an intermediary unit. The
> State is essentially a union of families, for being
> a permanent organisation it must, in its essential

constitution, provide for its own continuance,
which, according to the natural law, can be realised only through the medium of the family.[1]

Moreover, in discussing the family we should not focus exclusively on the nuclear family, that is, the immediate family
formed of a husband, wife and their children. Although
that is certainly the basis of the family and family life, the
existence and strength of the extended family does much to
promote a healthy social life, both directly and indirectly, and
for many centuries the extended family was simply assumed
as the normal and ordinary form of the family.[2]

An excellent framework for our discussion of the family is
the Charter of Family Rights from the apostolic exhortation
Familiaris Consortio (November 22, 1981) of Pope John Paul
II. Therefore in the first section of this chapter I will list each
of the statements from the Charter and use each statement
as the basis for the discussion that follows. One important
matter should be discussed at the outset, however. This is
the role and function of the state in providing for the needs
enumerated in the Charter. The shade of liberal opinion that
upholds the rigor and purity of the free market (those whom
we in the United States usually call conservatives) tends to say
that the state should have little or no role in these matters,
that they are best left to private, for-profit enterprises. The
more statist liberals, on the other hand, are apt to see in
each of them an opportunity for a new government bureau,
which will try to solve the problem directly. For example,
in the provision of health insurance, one side argues that
private individuals, with no motive other than greed, will

---

1 *The Framework of a Christian State*, p. 320.
2 For example, by caring for their aged members, an extended family
can perform an important function that otherwise many might wish
to transfer to the state.

adequately provide for society's needs; the other wants a new government program. The better approach, which is also the Catholic approach, sees the state's function to be this: "directing, supervising, encouraging, restraining, as circumstances suggest or necessity demands."[3] That is, the state has an important task in such matters, but it is ordinarily not one of directly providing a service itself, but rather of seeing that someone else is doing so, *fairly and efficiently*. And this someone else is more likely to be a mutual aid society or a cooperative, than a for-profit business, for the Catholic mind is as well aware of the dangers of greed as it is aware of the natural solidarity of mankind. With this in mind, let us turn to the Charter of Family Rights.

• *The right to exist and progress as a family, that is to say, the right of every human being, even if he or she is poor, to found a family and to have adequate means to support it.*

In the discussion of economics in chapter three, I pointed out that economic activity could be understood only if one attended to its purpose; that to look at such activity as simply a complex of individual actions with only the motives that each individual actor in this process has, is to gravely misunderstand why man has the need and capacity for economic activity. Similarly here we must look at the purpose of the human desire of marrying and founding a family. To say, for example, that if one is sufficiently poor then one has no right to marry, or at least to have children, is to look only at the individual's desires as if such desires were no more profound or significant than someone's yearning for a vacation home or a speedboat. In fact, God has put a desire for marriage into man's heart for very important social reasons. By creating us in the way that he did, God signified to a great degree how

3   Encyclical *Quadragesimo Anno*, no. 80.

we were to live; that is, by creating us as social beings who are entirely helpless during our early years, God clearly shows the necessity for both society (including a political order) and the family. And since what God does for us on one level does not frustrate what he does on another, but rather usually helps fulfill it, our own persons are completed by this also. All of us are dependent on society and on a family. Even if in some cases a person is not begotten or raised in a family, still the family is the norm. And if this ethical norm ceases to be the statistical norm, we will see just how dependent society's well-being is on the family. But perhaps more importantly, for most of us, life within society and within a family — or the quasi-family of a religious community — also fulfills the potentialities present in our own personalities and provides us with opportunities for perfecting ourselves. Thus the desire to marry and to found a family signifies much more than one's desire for a particular material good or gratification, since it flows from the depths of our nature as God created us.

If this is so, than obviously poverty or lack of means should not be allowed to prevent one from marrying or having a family. There seem to be two ways of addressing this. One is for the government or some intermediary body, or even the Church, to supply what is needed to the individuals who desire to marry so that poverty does not burden them in their family life and in the raising of their children. The second way, which I think is preferable, is for the laws and institutions of society to be such that poverty aside from exceptional circumstances would not exist. Some would still be richer than others, of course, but if the kind of economy sketched in chapter three existed, then no one would lack what was necessary for living a life worthy of a human person.[4]

4 The Irish Constitution (Article 45, clause 2) states, "The State shall, in particular, direct its policy towards securing: (i) That the citizens . . .

However, even in the most just of economies there will be times when for one reason or another, individuals or families are reduced to poverty. In such cases direct aid on the part of the state authorities is not only acceptable but required. As Pius XI taught in *Casti Connubii,*

> Wherefore, those who have the care of the State and of the public good cannot neglect the needs of married people and their families, without bringing great harm upon the State and on the common welfare. Hence, in making the laws and in disposing of public funds they must do their utmost to relieve the needs of the poor, considering such a task as one of the most important of their administrative duties. (no. 121)

But if an economy is oriented toward the common good and functioning as it should be, one hopes such occasions would be few. In some cases, as in someone disabled or a widow with children, long-term arrangements would have to be made, and the state must see to it that someone is there to take care of these kinds of needs, and always in a manner that respects the dignity and personality of the individual who is being helped.

• *The right to exercise its responsibility regarding the transmission of life and to educate children.*

Here one is concerned with a government's interference with a married couple's right, first, to exercise responsibility before God for the size of their family, and secondly, to be masters of the education of their children. In regard to both these points, obviously a Catholic state, as long as it remained

---

may through their occupations find the means of making reasonable provision for their domestic needs."

Catholic, would interfere with neither. As to the state's role in the first matter, it would protect married couples by prohibiting the manufacture or importing of contraceptive or abortifacient devices or chemicals. I believe that a state should make information on natural family planning widely available, always keeping in mind the moral principles that must accompany its use. However, no state could teach natural family planning and then demand that couples limit the number of their children.

What of situations in which a particular country or region were truly overcrowded, could in those circumstances a government organize a *non-coercive* campaign to promote natural family planning, without in any way penalizing those who chose to have large families? Could it be that the command of Almighty God in Genesis, "Be fruitful and multiply, and fill the earth. . . . " (1:28) might be considered accomplished if the earth really were fully populated as far as living in a reasonable human manner is concerned? It is true that the earth is not presently full, and at the time of writing birth rates are actually falling in most places, but speaking theoretically, if one country were fully populated and its neighbors did not permit extensive immigration, then it seems to me it would not be unjust for a government to initiate such a non-coercive campaign for natural family planning. The *Catechism of the Catholic Church* seems to address and approve such a situation when it says (no. 2372) that the state may "intervene to orient the demography of the population. This can be done by means of objective and respectful information, but certainly not by authoritarian, coercive measures."[5]

---

[5] John XXIII had touched on this subject in *Mater et Magistra*, nos. 185–195. See also *Populorum Progressio*, no. 37 and *Sollicitudo Rei Socialis*, no. 25.

Another matter, important at this time, is that it would be well if the government encouraged the practice of breast-feeding babies and young children. One would hope that a Catholic culture would support this eminently human and Christian act, which not only is good for the baby's and the mother's health, but also in many cases provides a period of natural infertility for couples. And in cases where for any reason such a healthy cultural activity is being eroded, it is just and fitting for the state — or the physicians' occupational group — to step in and, for example, require that a mother receive a physician's prescription in order to feed her baby with prepared formula.

As regards the education of children, the state must see its function as one of assisting parents. Thus the state should see that there are sufficient schools and universities for its population, but this does not mean that the state itself must directly provide these institutions. Direct and indirect aid to the Church or to groups of laymen or to the parents of students should be the ordinary means, and only if there is a need that is not being met by others' initiatives should the government directly establish its own schools.[6] And as I said in a previous chapter, it seems clear to me that the state should see that no one is hindered by poverty from receiving as much education as he can truly master, by providing scholarships and other aid.

While speaking of education, it might be well to discuss the question of universal and compulsory education. Today it is deemed exceedingly important that every adult be able

---

6   Fr. Cahill's opinion on this seems to parallel exactly my own. "As to the schools themselves the State should begin by encouraging and assisting good private schools, due to the initiative of the Church or the parents. State schools are to be set up only where private schools and those of the Church are found to be insufficient." *The Framework of a Christian State*, pp. 362–63.

to read and write. And in the present circumstances, this certainly seems justified since one needs to be able to read for nearly every job, to use public transportation, drive, etc. But, since I am writing for any state at any time, it is well to consider this question in the abstract.

In his delightful and prophetic book, *Survivals and New Arrivals*,[7] Hilaire Belloc had some very interesting words on this matter which I think bear repeating.

> According to [the Catholic conception of human nature], the first, the most necessary thing, is the teaching of the children, affirmatively, as a divine truth necessary not only to the conduct of its own life, but also to that of all society, the doctrines and the particular, defined, morals of the Catholic Church.

In comparison with instruction in that one prime essential, nothing else counts. It is good to be able to read and write and cast up simple sums; it is better still to know something of the past of one's people, and to have a true idea of the world around one. But these are nothing compared with the Faith.

A little later he notes,

> It is not without significance that the claim to interfere by force not only in the all-important character of early instruction, but in a score of other domestic things, has gone side by side with the spread of fatalism in the world and with the inhuman concept of unalterable mechanical laws. It is not insignificant that the Church in the rare places and times when She had power to do so, did

---

7 New York: Macmillan, 1929. The passages quoted are on pages 155–157 and page 165. The entire section on compulsory education runs from page 154 to 167.

not comple [sic] the mind. During all that intense intellectual life of the thirteenth century instruction was by choice: *endowed* — so that the poorest could reach the highest inspiration, but at the choice of the individual or family will, to be taken or left.

Then a few pages later he makes the following striking comment,

Here is an example: the attitude of the "Modern Mind" to illiteracy. The chief subjects of elementary instruction are reading and writing. Therefore a weakness or incapacity in these two departments becomes the test of inferiority. One nation may build, sing, paint, fight, better than another; but if it has a larger proportion unable to read, it is branded as the lesser of the two. A Spaniard of Estremadura may carve stone images as living as those of the thirteenth century, but if he cannot read, the "Modern Mind" puts him far below the loafer picking out racing tips in his paper.

It seems to me that what Belloc says here makes much sense. Insofar as schooling helps bring to actuality the various human potentialities, so much the better. If it enables us to know about God and the things of God, about the world and man in the light of the Faith, again, so much the better. But just as many other things can actualize his potentialities, e.g., a living tradition of art or oral poetry or music, so being able to read can simply mean that one will pass one's idle time reading worthless matter that tends to weaken and destroy both mind and soul. How many in industrial societies today spend time reading trash whose illiterate ancestors may have spent their time singing those old ballads or telling the tales that are some of the treasures of the different cultures of mankind?

In practice, moreover, compulsory schooling has often been seen as benefiting neither children nor their families, but the state. As one American public school official put it in 1912, "The schools exist primarily for the benefit of the State rather than for the benefit of the individual."[8] And though it is not wrong for a government to wish to make a nation strong, those who govern must always remember that the rulers of the state exist for the sake of the people, not vice versa.

Absence of compulsory schooling, then, would be the ideal, *when it is possible*, such as in an agricultural society. But when this is not feasible for any reason, a Catholic state would do well to include in its constitution or basic law the right of parents to home school their children, as the Irish constitution does in Article 42, clause 2.[9]

• *The right to the intimacy of conjugal and family life*

In this regard the most important thing that can be done for the family is to make it possible for fathers to have work, and to have work near where their wives and children live. In many areas of the world there is not enough work for men in certain regions, and as a result they must travel and live at a distance from their wives and children. Obviously this produces stresses on the family and temptations for husbands and wives. This separation of the father—or even the mother!—from the family also results from the capitalist economy which requires some workers, such as salesmen, to travel about, again creating this same problem. The solution to these problems lies in creating a just economy in which

---

8   Quoted in Allan Carlson, *From Cottage to Work Station* (San Francisco: Ignatius, 1993), p. 19. This book has a short but revealing account of the compulsory schooling movement in the United States on pages 18–20.

9   "Parents shall be free to provide this education in their homes or in private schools or in schools recognized or established by the State."

decentralized production and consumption eliminate as much as possible the need for workers to spend long periods of time away from their families.

• *The right to the stability of the bond and of the institution of marriage*

The state will be able to render great help to the institution of marriage and to each and every married couple, help which will promote their temporal and their eternal happiness, by prohibiting completely divorce. In fact, there is no reason for the state to have power over the marriages of Catholics at all, for the state has no rights over such marriages.[10] To quote Fr. Cahill again:

> The legitimate extent of civil authority in regard to Christian marriage is limited to two functions, namely, to safeguard, and, when necessary, to enforce the rights of the parties, and, secondly, to regulate and define certain civil consequences or accompaniments of marriage, concerning such matters as property and inheritance. Any unauthorized action of the State beyond these limits is an act of tyranny and usurpation, and tends directly to the degradation and ruin of human society.[11]

Thus in a Catholic state, when Catholics marry, the parish priest will simply send notification of this fact to an appropriate office of the state, so that the civil effects, for example, property rights, can be adjusted to take account of the married state of the persons involved. But the priest will not be acting

---

10 "Neither, therefore, by reasoning can it be shown, nor by any testimony of history be proved, that power over the marriages of Christians has ever lawfully been handed over to the rulers of the State." Leo XIII, Encyclical *Arcanum Divinae Sapientiae*, no. 24.
11 *The Framework of a Christian State*, pp. 346–47.

as the agent of the state in witnessing the marriage, and the registration of the marriage with the state will be after the fact of the marriage, i.e., it will be simply a notation that the marriage has occurred. The state will be taking cognizance of something that happened under the Church's jurisdiction, but which also concerns the civil authorities because of such matters as property, inheritance, etc. If this is done, then ecclesiastical courts alone will deal with questions involving declarations of nullity. Despite the fact that such courts in some eras and places, including our own, have been subject to abuses in granting annulments, nevertheless, they are the correct tribunals to govern Catholic marriages, rather than civil courts.

The state could permit those who adhere to other religions to contract marriages according to their own religious rites, if their religious doctrines do not violate the natural law in this regard, as for example, by allowing divorce or polygamy. Or, conceivably, it could require civil marriage for non-Catholics. Certainly there would have to be some provision for civil marriage for non-believers, unless it was judged wiser to simply allow marriage according to the natural law for them. In this case, couples, after having contracted marriage according to the natural law, that is, by mutual and free consent to a lifelong and exclusive union, could register their marriage with the state in order to give effect to property and inheritance rights. In such cases registration would also prevent pretended divorce or bigamy, since individuals attempting to register another marriage while their spouse was still living would be discovered.

• *The right to believe in and profess one's faith and to propagate it.*
• *The right to bring up children in accordance with the family's own traditions and religious and cultural values, with the necessary instruments, means and institutions.*

These two rights have been discussed in chapter two, which dealt with religious liberty. I only reiterate here that the family will have freedom to raise its children according to the religion of the parents, and freedom to use the "instruments, means and institutions" that are placed at their disposal by the state and society, e.g., educational funds and grants, as they see fit.

• *The right, especially of the poor and the sick, to obtain physical, social, political and economic security*
• *The right to housing suitable for living family life in a proper way*

I pointed out in chapter three that the purpose of economic activity is to supply the material goods needed by every individual and family, so that they can concentrate on things of more importance, such as their spiritual, intellectual, family and social lives. So, here again, the question is of the general justice of the economy, an economy structured so that each individual and head of family is able to work in dignity, to receive from his work sufficient for a decent human and family life, with freedom from inordinate cares, so that he and his family can devote their time to those things that are more important. Obviously this includes provision for adequate housing, and here, as in education, the state has the responsibility to oversee the situation and do what is necessary — usually indirectly, but directly if need be — so that people do not lack this housing.

The best way is simply for the economy to be arranged in such a way that even the poor have amply enough so that they themselves can provide for their own housing, as well as for all their ordinary expenses and needs. In this connection, since Pope John Paul speaks of the sick, I might mention the question of medical care. And here, I think, a distinction is in order between what might be called ordinary care and what is sometimes called in the United States catastrophic care, i.e., major illnesses or accidents, long hospital stays, expensive tests or surgeries, etc. No one can be expected to pay for costly catastrophic care out of his income or savings, so here some system of insurance is clearly necessary. A national government system is one possible way, and in some circumstances it might be the best, especially in a poor country; otherwise the various occupational groups, or a confederation of all occupational groups, or non-profit mutual aid societies, might provide such insurance to their members and their families, or perhaps a parish based system might work the best in other cases. What is important to remember is that no one type of system is always the best, and although Catholic tradition would favor a type run by some intermediary group, such as an occupational group, it would not say that a state system could never be the best choice. Nor is there anything wrong with more than one type of system in a country. For example, the unemployed might be directly insured by the state, while others would have their insurance through an occupational group. If some occupational groups were too small or poor to provide insurance, perhaps multiple groups could combine for this purpose, or the state could offer these groups assistance. But the point here is that the Catholic mind does not insist on only one approach to the matter or on one type of provider.

Of course, the alternatives to a government-provided national insurance plan, such as I suggested just now, assume a more stable society, and might not work as well in a society in which people frequently move around physically or change jobs so often as is the case now, especially in the highly-mobile society of the United States. But if we are to consider this matter theoretically, then it is necessary to mention these kinds of alternative approaches.

Moreover, there is nothing wrong, of course, in medical insurance schemes covering even routine physician's visits. In fact, in the early twentieth century in the United States some fraternal lodges or societies included medical care as part of the benefits offered to members.

> Two of the most prominent organizations to rely on this system, known at the time as lodge practice, were the Foresters and the Fraternal Order of Eagles. The cost of this service was very low. The Foresters charged two dollars a year for a doctor's care, and the Eagles charged one dollar. In the case of the Eagles, coverage extended to the immediate family of the member and included home visits.[12]

A few fraternal societies even had their own hospitals or hospitalization programs.[13]

• *The right to expression and to representation, either directly or through associations, before the economic, social and cultural public authorities and lower authorities*
• *The right to form associations with other families and institutions, in order to fulfill the family's role suitably and expeditiously*

These issues are discussed in chapter six, on democracy.

• *The right to protect minors by adequate institutions and legislation from harmful drugs, pornography, alcoholism, etc*

---

12   David T. Beito, "Fraternal Societies as an Alternative to the Welfare State" in Jeffrey J. Sikkenga, ed., *Transforming Welfare: the Revival of American Charity* (Grand Rapids, Mich.: Acton Institute, 1997), pp. 36–37.

13   *Ibid.*, p. 37. See also Bertram B. Fowler, *The Co-operative Challenge* (Boston: Little, Brown, 1947), pp. 182–194. The American Medical Association was hostile both to physicians contracting with fraternal societies and with cooperative medical plans. (See Beito, p. 38 and Fowler, pp. 185–188.)

This right goes without saying, but perhaps one should point out that, without the support of a culture, such laws are generally in vain. Thus the state will have to do more than simply outlaw harmful drugs, for example. By its watchful care of the economy, by its censorship laws, by its entire oversight of the common good, the state will strive to create the conditions in which a healthy culture can thrive, so that in turn the culture will make the state's laws fruitful and effective. It is the culture, not the legal system, that must bear most of the weight of safeguarding individuals and families in this matter.

• *The right to wholesome recreation of a kind that also fosters family values*

For the most part, the exercise of this right depends on families having the resources, including sufficient time, to obtain fitting recreation, and thus the problem is the same one treated of in chapter three, namely, how to insure economic justice in the nation for individuals and families, and the means discussed in that chapter, naturally, will apply here. And as is the case with education, the state will provide what is fitting, as, for instance, parks. One would hope, moreover, that a healthy Catholic culture would discourage the misuse of recreational activities, such as the commercialization of sports. Here again, an emphasis on localism in economic and popular culture would be important in preventing such abuses.

• *The right of the elderly to a worthy life and a worthy death*

One would hope that in a Catholic culture the elderly would rarely be placed in nursing homes or otherwise separated from their children and families. Again, economic issues are important here, for the aged need enough to live on, and families need enough so that care for their elders is not economically or socially burdensome. If individuals and extended families own productive property, then this will help supply such needs, and what I said above about catastrophic insurance obviously applies here also. Of course, any culture worthy of the name Catholic, would accord to the elderly some of that respect and honor which our ancestors were accustomed to render to them.

• *The right to emigrate as a family in search of a better life*
No sensible nor just Catholic state will ever constrain any person or family wishing to leave the country. Aside from the injustice to the family, as St. John Paul here notes, it is folly to prevent persons dissatisfied with the regime from leaving, for that simply allows a cancer of dissent to grow in the bowels of the nation.

II

Elsewhere I have argued that the kind of technology that a society has is a matter of great moment, and particularly is this true for a Christian society.[14] Technology is not neutral, merely something that can be used for good or evil but that of itself has no influence. Rather, it seems obvious that the kind of technology we use in a society has immense influence over how that society lives and even how that society thinks and perceives reality. Now I do not say that technology forces us to live or to think in a certain way; simply that, given our propensity to take the easy way out and to follow the path of least resistance, this is the case. To take but one instance out of many, the automobile makes it easy for small towns and

---

14 I have dealt with canons for the licit use of technology at length in chapter two of *The Catholic Milieu*. See also the volume which I edited, *The Glory of the Cosmos: A Catholic Approach to the Natural World*.

rural areas to lose the stores and other institutions that make up their economic base. With the automobile it becomes easy to drive to the nearest large town to shop in order to find a little wider selection or a little cheaper prices. As stores in villages close, this helps to depopulate them, as well as turn them into simply collections of residences, bedroom communities for the large towns where the jobs and stores are. Before the automobile, people could always travel if they really wanted to, if they had reason, but now we can drive off with hardly a second thought. Similarly in cities, not just the automobile but all modern means of transportation have made it possible for people to live miles from their place of work, contributing to the sprawl of the suburbs into the countryside, the building of gigantic and now overcrowded highway systems, and, of course, the separation of family from work, an important part of the disunity of today's life.

Moreover, this has affected how we think too, as I said. When we plan cities or new roads or new factories or anything, we assume the use of the automobile and the separation of work from home. We look on a stable community as a stagnant pond instead of as a solid oak tree, growing and content in its own place. We cannot really imagine a world without the automobile. But if we truly value community and detest the atomization of modern life, then it seems to me that we must regret the invention of the car.[15]

But even should one disagree with me on the specific question of the automobile, I still insist on the general principle that technology can sometimes do evil to a society and a people. And if this is true, then the question arises, should

---

15   The best indictment of the automobile that I have ever seen appeared in George Kennan's book, *Around the Cragged Hill: a Personal and Political Philosophy* (New York: Norton, 1993). It seems to me difficult to praise Kennan's remarks on the automobile too highly.

a Catholic state formulate laws dealing with technology, perhaps seek to regulate inventions for the common good? The answer to this question depends upon many things, including the technological state of the country when a Catholic regime is instituted. In some cases it might be wise to have some kind of official board which judges new inventions. Obviously in other situations such a board would be ludicrous, but there are some actions that I think can be done in any situation. First, refuse to erect artificial spurs to invention, such as patent laws, which encourage indiscriminate inventions regardless of their merits and the needs of society.[16] Secondly and more importantly, attempt to diffuse throughout the society a spirit which, instead of welcoming everything new, attempts to judge whether new things truly serve the purpose of technology, namely, whether they allow us to devote more of our time and energy to our spiritual, intellectual, family and social lives *without injuring the social body or the environment in any way.*[17] If they do, then admit them to the state;

---

16   In Mark Twain's novel, *A Connecticut Yankee in King Arthur's Court*, the hero, "a nineteenth-century technical Yankee" who manages to establish a "benevolent dictatorship" over sixth-century Britain, says that the establishment of a patent office was the first act of his rule. "The very first official thing I did, in my administration ...was to start a patent office; for I knew that a country without a patent office and good patent laws was just a crab, and couldn't travel any way but sideways or backways." Quoted in Richard Hofstadter, *Anti-intellectualism in American Life* (New York: Alfred A. Knopf, 1964), p. 242.

17   Consider these words of Pius XII, from his Christmas message of 1957, "Technical progress, on the other hand, when it imprisons man within its own narrow confines, cuts him off from the rest of the universe, especially the world of the spiritual and of the inner man, and forms him according to its own characteristics, the most noteworthy of which are superficiality and instability. The way this kind of deformation comes about is no secret to anyone who is aware of man's tendency to accept false judgments and errors as long as they hold out the promise of an easier life. Take for example the questionable substitution of values that has taken place as a result of the

if not, do not admit them. I realize that to many the notion
of controlling technology is, to say the least, novel, but if we
admit that technology affects how we live, how can we afford
to do nothing? Unless we are to lose all control over such an
important aspect of the common good, we cannot afford to
adopt a laissez-faire attitude here.[18] Nor do I insist that the
remedies I have suggested are always the appropriate ones.
But I do insist that the issue is real, and that the guardians
of the temporal common good cannot neglect it if they wish
to preserve the health of the culture. For, just as in artistic
creation, not everything that comes from the hand of fallen
man is truly for his good.

---

wonderful progress made in the speed of machines. The 'speed-crazy'
man is attracted by this progress and easily carries his high regard
for speed over to things whose proper development and value do
not depend on rapid change, but rather on stability and fidelity to
traditions." Quoted in John Cronin, *Social Principles and Economic
Life* (Milwaukee: Bruce, 1959), pp. 8–9.

Since the first edition of this book, the notable encyclical of Pope
Francis, *Laudato Si'*, appeared in May 2015. It is an excellent approach
to the question of the environment and technology based on sound
Catholic thinking.

18   St. Thomas endorses Plato's opinion that products of an art
"which for the most part some people put to an evil use, although such
arts are not unlawful in themselves ... should be extirpated from the
State by the governing authority." (*Summa Theologiae* II–II q. 169,
a. 2, ad obj. 4)

Fanfani, in his work already referred to several times, *Catholicism,
Protestantism and Capitalism*, avers that "in a perfectly Catholic age
purely technical progress would not have found such powerful incen-
tives as in a capitalistic civilization," because the economic stimu-
lus would not operate in such an unfettered manner in seeking ever
increasing profits. See p. 141.

6

Democracy

> It is easy enough to argue that the mob makes mistakes; but as a fact it never has a chance even to make mistakes until its superiors have used their superiority to make much worse mistakes.
>
> — G. K. Chesterton.[1]

I

T WOULD BE A FOOLISH ENTERPRISE to attempt to discuss the form of government that a Catholic state should have, because it is clear that this is pretty much an indifferent matter, or to speak more strictly, a matter in part indifferent and in part a result of historical and cultural circumstances. Who could imagine a king of Switzerland, for example? And Leo XIII's teaching on this in the encyclical *Immortale Dei* and elsewhere is well-known, that "no one of the several forms of government is in itself condemned, inasmuch as none of them contains anything contrary to Catholic doctrine, and all of them are capable, if wisely and justly managed, to insure the welfare of the State" (no. 36).[2] This chapter, then, is not an evaluation of different forms of government, or even a critique of the strengths and weaknesses of democracy as we know it today in the West, that is, representative democracy operating with a full panoply of political parties, lobbyists, public opinion polls and pressure groups, amply chronicled and dissected,

---

1 "The Common Man" in *The Common Man* (London: Sheed and Ward, 1950), p. 6.
2 This teaching is also contained in *Immortale Dei*, no. 4 and *Diuturnum*, nos. 6–7.

sometimes even fairly, by the news media. Instead what I am attempting in this chapter is to discuss what is permanently important and necessary in the idea of democracy, or, more correctly, in popular participation in ruling—what sort of popular participation ought to exist in every state and type of regime, whether republic or monarchy, representative democracy or otherwise.

Since this is the age of liberal democracy, in which even most of its enemies give it lip service, doubtless it seems that no other form of government will ever replace it in the esteem of the learned or of the people. But I do not think that this is necessarily so, and I would not be surprised to see democracy discredited, even in my lifetime. I do not say that this is good or bad, simply that I expect it eventually to take place. And the reason that I expect this, is that our kind of democracy, like any kind of political regime, is dependent on a particular culture. A contemporary writer has stated this well:

> Liberal democracy which pretends to universalism is historically specific. It is a child of industrial civilization, a product of a socially atomized society where production and exchange are already commodified, a society which is essentially a market. It is the product of a society in which interests are so particularized that the very notion of common interest becomes problematic, hence the imperative of democracy.[3]

---

3 Claude Ake, "The Unique Case of African Democracy," *International Affairs*, vol. 69, no. 2 (April 1993), pp. 242–243.

Another reason why we might not expect democracy to last forever can be found in the teaching of more than one ancient author that, as Plato put it, "tyranny is probably established out of no other regime than democracy, I suppose — the greatest and most savage slavery out of the extreme of freedom" (*Republic* 564a, Allan Bloom translation). Plato's entire argument in the *Republic* (557a to 566d) about how

Now the extent to which such a "socially atomized society" could be a Catholic society, and hence, the extent to which modern representative democracy fits in well with a Catholic civilization, is not under discussion here. Rather, as I said, I want to point out some elements connected with popular rule which, it seems to me, are not only fully compatible with a Catholic regime, but essential for any healthy state.

Let me begin with two quotations.

> The medieval king was not absolute. True, the faculty of legislation belonged to the Crown: *quod principi placuit vim legit habet* (the king's pleasure has the force of law). But already in the Visigothic period the famous legal code, the *Fuero Juzgo*, had laid it down that the king was king only if he did right (*Rex eris si recte facias: si non facias, non eris*). In Spain as elsewhere in Europe the first and most fundamental principle of medieval political thought was that all political authority was the expression of justice. The second great principle was that there could be only one source of political authority: the community or the people itself. The King of Castile or Aragon had two superiors, God and the Law—law not made by the prince or legislator,

---

democracy tends to decline into tyranny should not be discounted just because it is old. Josef Pieper's discussion of this is also worth noting; see *The Four Cardinal Virtues*, pp. 92–96.

In *Europe and the Faith* (reprinted by TAN Books, 1992), Hilaire Belloc comments on the 16th and 17th-century enthusiasm for absolute monarchy (pp. 161–163). Our own age has a similar feeling for democracy. We simply cannot imagine how any other form of government could ever be just or desirable.

Between the first edition of this book and now I think it is fair to say that already we can see a certain decline in the intellectual hegemony of democracy, if not in North America and western Europe, at least in other parts of the world.

but expressing the habit and custom of the community's life.[4]

And my second is a familiar dictum, usually attributed to Abraham Lincoln: "You can fool all the people some of the time and some of the people all of the time, but you can't fool all of the people all of the time."

What do these two quotations teach us about democracy — or popular government — that is permanently valuable? The first quote sets forth a notion of government in which the rulers are, above all, to respect the traditions held by the people, the traditions of the community. Moreover, if the king (in this case) did not act rightly, he had forfeited his right to rule. The king was answerable not to a complex political process, a system of checks and balances, able to be manipulated by those with cunning or power, but to a few simple facts: Did he violate justice? Did he betray the traditions of the people? If he did do these things, perhaps he could still cling to power, but everyone knew he was in reality no longer king.

The Lincoln quote recognizes the fact that the people cannot always be taken in by the schemes of their rulers — and this includes not just political and military schemes but new schemes of morality, new and revolutionary ways of living, in short, whatever goes counter to the traditions of a nation and people. Common sense may be uncommon in individuals, but taken in the mass, it will be present, at least often: " . . . you can't fool all of the people all of the time." And the more that a people has been able to keep their traditions, the more they have tenaciously clung to their traditional wisdom,

---

4 J. B. Trend, *The Civilization of Spain* (London: Oxford University, 1944, 1960 printing), p. 63. See also Bede Jarrett, *Social Theories of the Middle Ages*, pp. 29–30, 132–133, and St. Thomas Aquinas, *De Regimine Principum*, chapter 6.

then the more they will have this common sense that can be a corrective to the schemes or delusions of their rulers.

Thus it seems to me that both these quotes, in different ways, can teach us that in any type of regime there is a necessary function of popular government, and that that function is a conservative one — using that word without any ideological or philosophical meaning. Simply that in any society with traditions, which would include most societies, the customs and beliefs of the people are the true depository of those traditions. Thus real popular government is one which is in accord with the deepest traditions and beliefs of the people, and which respects those traditions and beliefs, whether or not that government is a formal democracy in either the modern or the classical sense. Government must be prevented from outraging these most basic beliefs and traditions. Whether that can best be prevented by a formal representative democracy or by some other system is a decision of political prudence that each state must make. But as a general rule there are many different ways a state can solve this problem, and moreover there are many ways to provide a formal mechanism for a popular voice in governing.

Since the early modern period there has been in the Western world a growing gulf between what was held by the various elites of the culture and what was held by the common people.[5] Of course not all members of the elites were alienated from their civilization's roots, but increasingly this was the case. In such cases their aim has been to persuade and hoodwink the people into accepting a philosophy which may be said to have achieved its mature consciousness with the so-called Enlightenment of the 18th century.[6] And despite

---

5 This gulf has been harmful both for the people and for the elites. See *The Catholic Milieu*, pp. 39–48, for a discussion of this.
6 Chesterton's essay, "The Common Man" has many delightful

the fact that many of the regimes in which this has been done were formally democracies, the elites have accomplished their goal not by a full and frank discussion of the issues, but by obfuscation and deceit.[7] This has been made easier, moreover, because the traditions that are held by the people are not often held in the explicit manner that is susceptible of intellectual disputation. Thus they are peculiarly open to being confused and led astray by what can seem to be a complete and fair discussion, but in reality is selective and biased discourse. In this unfortunate cultural chasm between the elites and the people, the people are at a great disadvantage. Only rarely do genuine populists manage to organize sufficiently to seize control of what are supposed to be — in a democracy — the people's own institutions.

It is, however, inevitable, and in normal situations, good, that elites rule. This becomes a difficulty only when the intellectual elite has an outlook or philosophy that is antagonistic to that of the people, who ordinarily will hold that set of beliefs which is traditional to the civilization. But since what is traditional may also be erroneous, in whole or in part, it

---

comments on this historical process. It is a wonderful indictment of the modern Western elites who have engineered a "modern emancipation" that is really a "new persecution of the Common Man." p. 1. "Progress, in the sense of the progress that has progressed since the sixteenth century, has upon every matter persecuted the Common Man. . . ." pp. 4–5. The entire essay is a good complement to this chapter.

7   An entire cultural history of Europe and the Americas would be required in order to illustrate all the instances where this has been done. One current example must suffice, the campaign for homosexual rights in the United States. The issue has been framed as an instance of the denial of civil rights and of discrimination against a minority. The assumption (never made explicit) is that sexual inclination is an essentially trivial factor, such as skin color. Thus a discussion of the real issue is avoided, and people are cleverly duped into supporting what they are taught to perceive as an instance of the unjust denial of civil rights.

is necessary that there be fruitful interchange between the conserving factor in a culture — the common people — and that factor which ought to be seeking to purify and sift, in the interests of truth, the traditions of the culture, namely, the intellectual elite. But this purifying and sifting ought to be done from a sympathetic standpoint, not one of supercilious and smug mockery of the common people.

It would be out of place here to speak generally of the complex question of the function of this conservative force and this sifting force — complex, because in cultures whose traditions are false, there must be a means to allow the truth of the Gospel to enter, for example. But our concern here is only with Catholic cultures, and so I will discuss only the roles which, it seems to me, these two factors ought to play in such a culture, a culture in which the traditions, one presumes, would be basically sound.

What we should aim for is this: That since the people have a conserving function in a civilization, some mechanism should be devised to formalize this role, to make it more likely that if a crisis does erupt, the people can effectively protect their civilization's traditions. And although processes themselves can never guarantee good results, still they are necessary, because even with the best good will, sufficient evil is always with us so that we need some kind of formal means whereby we can defend our rights. Without going into detail, what possibilities can be sketched of formal means for the people to intervene in the political process in order, if the need arises, to restrain the elites from undermining the traditions of the nation? Obviously in a formal democracy this need is not supposed to arise, for such forms of government are supposed to reflect the desires of the people. Be that as it may, though, it would seem to be the case that the best method for preserving a Catholic people's traditions is the existence of institutions committed to the explicit defense of those traditions. Now the kinds of institutions that would be needed here would be as varied as the various traditions that were being defended. For example, the first attack on the Christian traditions of our culture did not concern sex or the family. The first attack (aside from the Protestant theological revolt) was on economic morality, yet it was similar to the current assault on the family. Many intellectuals embraced new theories about the proper organization of economic life, ownership, the place of free competition, self-interest and suchlike.[8] And as the assault began — as these new ideas were eagerly snatched up by the rich and by rulers — it turned out to be chiefly the small man that was the victim. His workshop was put out of business by larger firms, and in the country, under the new conception of ownership, his rural cousin found himself put off land on which his fathers had lived for centuries, but for which he himself had no clear individual title of ownership.

Now, how could the traditions and the rights of the people have been defended in these circumstances? More effective perhaps than representation in any parliament would have been powerful organizations which stood for the small man. And in fact such organizations did exist, at least for the urban dweller, namely, the guilds. But from the 16th century on the guilds everywhere grew weaker. This shows that no kind of institution or procedure can be an absolute guarantee, as I said before, but nevertheless I think it does point to the sort of safeguard for the interests of the people which would be most effective, namely, the establishment of numerous organizations standing for the rights of the people, organizations

8 "There was a sense in which 'liberal economics' were a proclamation of freedom, for the few who were rich enough to be free." Chesterton, "The Common Man," p. 4.

that were wealthy and powerful enough to fight even against
the government, if need arose. I spoke of such groups above
in chapter three, but here I wish to emphasize that they are
the best guardians of the true popular interest. Although
often the people do not have well-formed or well-founded
opinions on many political decisions that must be made,
those for example concerning the everyday conduct of foreign or economic policy, they do stand for their own deepest
traditions and beliefs. Moreover, very often they have the
sense not to be deluded into supporting the grandiose and
absurd projects that can fascinate their rulers. And although
the history of our era shows how populaces can be brought
onto the bandwagon to support all kinds of dubious wars,
yet they are most likely to be right and to be tenacious of
their rights when they are defending something of their own.
So not only guilds or occupational groups, but leagues and
family associations of all types should be established to jeal-
ously guard those rights.[9] These associations and institutions
can be the guardians of true democracy. They, it seems to
me, are at least as important as having a right to vote for a
representative who in turn will vote on hundreds of measures
about which both he and his constituents are ill-informed,
and the implications of which usually neither understands.
They are the protections for that common people whom one
cannot always fool and for the welfare of whom the state, its
rulers, and the learned themselves, primarily exist.

Moreover, it might be desirable for occupational groups,
family leagues, cooperatives, and other bodies to have

9 An interesting example of how true popular associations even
today can sometimes defend the traditions of the people against the
prevailing intellectual consensus is the labor union. In the United
States unions opposed the so-called equal rights amendment and
opposed communism after both of these positions had ceased to be
fashionable, i.e., had ceased to be supported by the intellectual elite.

representation themselves, if not in a parliament conceived after the modern manner, at least in some kind of assembly with certain veto rights over the projects and plans of the government.[10] For it might be that an arrangement could be established whereby representatives of the people — not necessarily elected on a "one man, one vote" scheme — or of organizations of the people, would have the right to disapprove some legislation of the government, especially that involving the chance of war, the expenditure of very large sums of money, the imposition of heavy or unusual taxes or a threat to the sound traditions and customs of the country. In any case, a true Catholic political sensibility will recognize the great importance of the many subordinate groups which arise in a healthy culture, and will look beyond the ideology of the 18th century when deciding upon what role to give those groups in the government and its policies.

As I said above, the exact mechanisms or kinds of institutions that ought to fulfill this role of protecting a Catholic

---

10 The Irish parliament operates in part according to such a principle, the upper house or seanad (senate) being composed of representatives of various social sectors and graduates of specific universities. Article 18 of the Irish constitution provides for three members of the seanad to be elected by the National University of Ireland and three by the University of Dublin. In addition the following social and economic sectors receive representation:

i. National Language and Culture, Literature, Art, Education and such professional interests as may be defined by law for the purpose of this panel;

ii. Agriculture and allied interests, and Fisheries;

iii. Labour, whether organized or unorganized;

iv. Industry and Commerce, including banking, finance, accountancy, engineering and architecture;

v. Public administration and social services, including voluntary social activities.

But this principle is considerably diluted, since the seanad has merely advisory powers, and is able only to delay legislation.

society's sound traditions and customs cannot be specified in the abstract, and even in a particular country or culture they might well change as new needs or threats arise. But, as I have so often said in this book, the thing must be done if a culture is to be kept healthy. Whether the threat comes from a king, a group of nobles, the rich, or a representative assembly of some kind, the common people must have some effective defense. Only if this conservative function of the people is strong and is able to check attacks made on its traditions, only then can the culture hope for stability and have a chance to endure.[11]

---

11 However, more than the conservative function of the common people is necessary in order to preserve the health of a Catholic culture. The intellectual elite also has an important role in keeping a culture sound. In the next chapter I sketch some of the means by which this may be done.

7

The Ultimate Preservatives of Catholic Life

I N THIS CHAPTER I WILL TAKE UP THE interesting question of what, in the long run, must be hoped for to preserve a Catholic culture in all its vitality and vibrant orthodoxy. In the last chapter I spoke of the conserving role of the common people in maintaining the Catholic character of a culture. And although this conserving function is necessary it is not sufficient to preserve a Catholic society in what should be a vigorous and fresh orthodoxy. Most of Europe, from the conversion of the Roman Empire till the 18th century, was more or less a Catholic culture and was supported by numerous kinds of Catholic states. Yet this Catholic culture tragically went into decline and has disappeared. And surely whatever new Catholic cultures might arise will again suffer decline and again perhaps disappear, for as the epistle to the Hebrews says, ". . . here we have no lasting city, but we seek the city which is to come" (13:14). But it is certainly also right for us to learn from what happened before and, as much as we can, provide effective safeguards for the future—if there is any future for a Catholic state and Catholic culture.

Now, in the first place, as is evident from the whole theme of this book, a Catholic state is a protector of Catholic culture and thus of Catholic life. At the same time a Catholic culture in its turn also preserves a Catholic state, for unless the Faith is a living reality for the rulers and thinkers of a Catholic state, it will very soon lose its Catholic character, as the old motto that laws are in vain without custom bears witness.[1]

The entire burden of this book has been about how a Catholic state can preserve a Catholic culture by being its external framework. But since it is the same people who will live within a Catholic culture and who will administer the Catholic state, which is the culture's civic framework, if they begin to lose the fervor of their faith, then both culture and state will decline together. A Catholic state is an important protection for the culture, but it cannot protect it against everything, especially against the slow, dry rot of decaying faith or zeal. But is there anything which can protect a Catholic culture from within, as it were, anything which we can foster which will make it more probable that a particular Christian civilization will stand against the decline in faith and fervor and charity that has so often afflicted Catholics?

There are two things, I think, that, we must rely on if there is any hope of the preservation of a Catholic civilization. The two things are an intellectual formation and the cultivation of the interior life. And both of these involve the formation of a select group of persons within society. Before discussing exactly what I propose here I will speak in general of how each of these can act to protect a Christian culture.

First, an *intellectual formation*. An understanding and acceptance of the intellectual principles that underlie and flow from the Faith is absolutely essential in a Catholic culture. I do not say that this is necessary in the same way for everyone, but the more who fully grasp these principles the better. It is never sufficient that we hold the Faith merely

---

1 Cf. Horace, *Odes*, book 3, no. 24, line 35, *Quid leges sine moribus vanae proficiunt?*

as something traditional that has been passed on from our fathers nor that we make a blind Protestant-like leap of faith when we accept the revelation of Jesus Christ. Although we must, of course, take care that we do not reduce the Faith to a philosophy, something which is merely commended by our reason as the correct explanation of reality, still Catholics must be able to justify their religion on the intellectual plain (see I Peter 3:15.). Moreover, this is not just something we need to do for the sake of unbelievers, but for ourselves and our children also. In the long run a civilization that cannot rationally account for its most basic theological and philosophical tenets is doomed to lose them, for rational criticism will eventually undermine them. Thus a Protestant civilization can never last, but a Catholic civilization *should* be able to, for we can give this rational defense.

An equally important reason for grasping the intellectual principles of the Faith is that this is necessary if the Faith is to be kept pure, and especially if the judgments we make based on the Faith are to be sound. For example, a Catholic state and a Catholic culture will need numerous laws, rules and customs, on everything from what books are permitted free circulation to what sorts of economic arrangements are judged compatible with the common good. In such matters it is very easy to make false judgments, both too lax and too strict, so it is vitally important that these decisions be, as much as possible, clearly deduced from first principles. For if a Catholic culture makes stupid restrictions on man's freedom this can go a long way to tear down and make ridiculous the Faith and a society based on the Faith. But if we understand what we are about, why we are Catholics and what the implications of the Faith really are, then we can judge our own institutions and customs with a sureness and calmness born of understanding and well thought-out principles.

Second, the *interior life*. Consider this passage from St. Pius X's favorite spiritual book:

> Infection from the ills of former ages could well enough be countered, and souls preserved in health, by a merely ordinary piety. But the virulence of the pestilence in our own times, a hundred times more deadly, and so quickly caught from the fatal attractions of the world, must be fought with a much more powerful serum. And because we have had no laboratories in which to produce any effective antitoxins, Catholic Action has either done little more than produce a certain fervor of the feelings, great spasms of enthusiasm which sputter out as quickly as they burst into flame, or else, in cases where it is effective in itself, Catholic Action has reached little more than a small minority. Our seminaries and novitiates have not turned out the armies of priests, religious, and nuns, inflamed with the wine of the Eucharist, that we might have expected from them. And therefore the fire which these chosen souls were supposed to spread among the pious laypeople engaged in Catholic Action has remained latent. No doubt some pious apostles have been given to the Church. But only very rarely has she received from us workers who possess by their Eucharistic lives that total, uncompromising holiness based on custody of the heart and on ardent, active, generous, and practical zeal, all of which goes by the name of the interior life.[2]

The interior life, that is, a life lived closely with our Lord and in which we judge of things, not by the world's standards but by God's, is the *sine qua non* of Catholic stability. Unless

---

2 Jean-Baptiste Chautard, *The Soul of the Apostolate* (Trappist, Kentucky: Abbey of Gethsemani, c. 1946), pp. 180–81.

we at least strive to attain such a life, and do all we can to approach it, all our Catholic activity will never be able to counteract the world. The overwhelming and tremendous power of modern life cannot be conquered by a piety that is content with half measures and looks on the Christian life with less than total dedication and zeal. But an interior life is founded, of course, ultimately on the Cross, that symbol of contradiction to the world. Yet for us, who acknowledge the life-giving power of that sacred wood, has not the reality of the Cross grown dim? Yes, we readily confess our Savior's cruel death on it, yet do we as readily embrace that Cross in our own lives? Do we embrace the crosses our Lord lovingly sends us, or do we turn away scandalized that God is demanding *this* of *me*! If so, then our attitude toward the Cross is really no different from that of the world. Yet not only can the modern world be overcome by nothing less than an interior life led with the Crucified, but only that kind of life will, in the long run, preserve a Catholic culture and a Catholic state. Only such a life can preserve a fresh and living culture, and prevent a Catholic state from deteriorating into perhaps a dreary dictatorship, a dictatorship, moreover, whose influence on the culture is nil, or even negative, since it simply stifles men's spirits and fosters cultural nihilism and intellectual rebellion.

Now, what exactly do I mean when I say that an intellectual formation and the interior life are necessary for the preservation of a Christian culture? First of all, I am not speaking simply of creating some kind of elite within the state, for the more widespread such an intellectual and spiritual formation is, the better. If everyone had the grasp of the Faith of a theologian and a philosopher and the life of a saint, so much the better. But since we know that not everyone will achieve a high intellectual or spiritual level, it seems to me essential that some achieve this, and that, without considering themselves superior beings, they serve as a kind of leaven in the lump, or, to change the metaphor, as the salt that will keep a culture fresh and alive. Thus the formation of select apostles by means of the interior life and a Christian intellectual formation is, I think, a necessary means to aid in the preservation of a Catholic culture and a Catholic state. What I have in mind is something like this.

I imagine a kind of loosely-knit society, made up of those who have been given an ample Christian intellectual and cultural formation,[3] and who, under the guidance of priests and others, are striving to live an interior life. The members could be recruited during university studies as well as other-wise — it should certainly be open to those of the working class — and formally admitted to the movement. The entire purpose of the movement would be to uphold the Catholic tone of the culture and of the state, first, on a personal and family level, secondly, in the wider society. This would take the form, not only of applying Christian principles to their work, but of watching for, and prudently correcting, nascent errors and problems. Their apostolate would include formal and informal teaching of others, in person and in writing, in order to permeate the popular mind with Christian principles,

---

3   By a "Christian intellectual and cultural formation" I do not mean something like a summer course or a short series of lectures. I mean something as extensive as a complete university course, or its equivalent. I think, though, that there should be some formal arrangement whereby those who did not receive a university education could receive this formation later on.

"Education for the apostolate presupposes an integral human education suited to each one's abilities and conditions.... Besides spiritual formation, solid grounding in doctrine is required: in theology, ethics and philosophy, at least, proportioned to the age, condition and abilities of each one." Vatican Council II, Decree on the Apostolate of Lay People, *Apostolicam Actuositatem*, no. 29.

not only for one's personal life, but for society as a whole, for entertainment and recreation, for making political judgments, for understanding world events.[4]

Such apostles, men and women, would certainly need to work in concert with the hierarchy, but it seems to me they should not become too dependent on it, since there are too many instances in Catholic history of the betrayal of a nation by its bishops. Moreover, I think it would be better for them as a group to have no official connection with the government, for if the authorities were ever to take any actions against the Faith or against sound morality, such an apostolic group would need to retain maximum freedom of action.

There is also a very important role for Catholic literature — novels, drama, films, music, and so on — to play in helping to preserve a Catholic culture, and in putting flesh, as it were, on the bones of theological and philosophical principles. This has both a positive and a negative side. On the positive side, to embody Catholic principles in the lives and struggles of fictional characters, to explore humanity's ideals, victories and defeats; and in the negative, to illustrate the effects of error and sin.

Literature does not teach by forming correct ideas and true propositions in us, but rather by forming our sensibilities in a Christian direction, for "literature presents the ideals of philosophy and religion in an attractive parable or fable to bring our heart, our weak human nature, into harmony with our head, our spirit."[5] In medieval and Baroque Europe and the Catholic regions of the New World there was an effective

---

4   An interesting book that gives an account of a similar sort of apostolate is Felix Morlion, O. P., *The Apostolate of Public Opinion* (Montreal: Fides, 1944).

5   App, *The True Concept of Literature*, p. 7.

use of this means, as popular drama presented not only the truths of the Faith, but our ever-present struggle with the world, the flesh, and the Devil.[6] Something like this is equally necessary today. Plays, films, stories, novels and songs which strive, not to teach didactically (something that is not the province of literature), but to present Christian truths in an appealing guise, and to do the opposite with error and vice. Most of us perhaps remember some passage from a book which has stuck with us and which renders vice — already attractive enough — yet more attractive, because of its sympathetic presentation. Literature's mission is to do that same thing with virtue.

Of course, merely pietistic works of fiction and melodramatic sentimentalism are hardly the ideal here. We must hope that a living Catholic culture will produce Catholic writers worthy of the name and aware of the cultural trends and needs of the times. If they do not arise, there is little that can be done to create them beyond such general support as literary workshops or fellowships.

These recommendations are important devices for preserving a culture. Will they always be successful? Hardly. But they both seem to me to correspond to human needs and the needs of a culture. Everything human, because of the effects of original sin, will always tend to run down and become corrupted, and only vigilant measures have any hope of succeeding against them. So let these and other measures be tried, with as much vigor as we can muster, and perhaps we will be more successful in preserving and prolonging a healthy Catholic civilization than we otherwise would be.

---

6   Bede Jarrett points out how the medieval artist was conceived as expressing, in the manner proper to his art, the truths taught by the theologian. *Social Theories of the Middle Ages*, pp. 250–251, 256–257.

APPENDIX I

A NOTE ON DISTRIBUTISM
AND SOLIDARISM

THERE HAVE BEEN TWO SERIOUS ATTEMPTS
to outline an economic system that would correspond with
the program set forth in papal encyclicals beginning with Leo
XIII's *Rerum Novarum* of 1891. These are solidarism[1] and distributism. Solidarism was formulated by a remarkable German
Jesuit, Heinrich Pesch (1854–1926). As a young seminarian
Pesch spent the years 1885 to 1888 near Liverpool in England
because Bismarck's *Kulturkampf* had driven religious orders
out of Germany. In England Pesch witnessed the exploitation
and degradation of the working class by industrial capitalism
which made him resolve to devote his life as a priest to the
social apostolate. He later studied economics at the University of Berlin and authored a number of books on the social
question, his chief work being the monumental *Lehrbuch der
Nationalökonomie*, which appeared in five volumes between
1905 and 1923. Pesch has been widely credited with being the
major influence on Pius XI's 1931 social encyclical, *Quadragesimo Anno*.

Distributism, on the other hand, is best known because of
two of its outstanding exponents, Hilaire Belloc (1870–1953)
and G. K. Chesterton (1874–1936), but in their own time

---

1   Sometimes a third system is suggested, corporatism, *corporation*
here meaning guild or occupational group, not corporation as that
term is used in Anglo-American law, where it denotes a limited liability
company. But in fact corporatism is virtually identical with solidarism
for which Pesch provided the exhaustive theoretical foundation.

there were numerous other distributist writers and activists, Catholic and non-Catholic, and organizations such as the Distributist League and the Catholic Land Movement. Although both Chesterton and Belloc were public intellectuals widely read in many branches of thought, and Belloc was a history graduate of Oxford University, unlike Pesch neither was a trained economist, and neither produced anything comparable to Pesch's scholarly economic writings. In addition to a multiplicity of articles, Chesterton's social thought is chiefly contained in three books, *What's Wrong With the World* (1910), *Utopia of Usurers and Other Essays* (1917), both written before his reception into the Catholic Church, and *The Outline of Sanity* (1926). Belloc's chief contributions to distribuist thought were *The Servile State* (1913), *Economics for Helen* (1924), and *The Restoration of Property* (1936), this last being a sketch of how a distributist economy might be established.[2]

Both solidarism and distributism were formulated in response to the new social and economic order created by capitalism and industrialism that had triumphed in Europe and elsewhere during the nineteenth century. What was unique in capitalism, or more correctly, in the classical liberalism that stood behind capitalism, was the notion that the economic order was divorced from its place in the hierarchy of values that had hitherto been seen as the organizing principle of social life as a whole. Economic life, and consequently

---

2   Many of the works of Pesch, Chesterton and Belloc are in print and available. Pesch's major works, as translated by Dr. Rupert Ederer have been published by the Edwin Mellen Press, and in addition a very useful volume of excerpts from the *Lehrbuch* is available from University Press of America. IHS Press publishes Pesch's *Ethics and the National Economy* as well as a generous selection of works of Chesterton, Belloc and other early distributists. Ignatius Press also sells editions of Chesterton's distributist writings.

greed for gain unconnected from any inherent end, were now seen as legitimate and free from all but the most rudimentary ethical restraints. Prohibitions against force and fraud, narrowly defined, were pretty much the only misdeeds which the apologists of the new order recognized.

Both distributism and solidarism, on the other hand, since they are rooted in Catholic social thought, perceive that the economy must serve mankind as a whole and that economic activity must be part of the hierarchy of human goods, not an independent thing divorced from its place in social life, to be pursued according to the desire and cleverness of each individual economic actor, motivated solely by a desire for unrestricted gain. Pesch stated this principle at the outset of the *Lehrbuch*, when he wrote that "man must always and everywhere be the subject and end of the economy."[3]

If solidarism and distributism are compared, one will find that the differences between them are chiefly a matter of emphasis. As such, they both witness to the fact that all serious attempts to apply Catholic social doctrine will necessarily resemble each other much more than they will differ. Both systems take their keynote from Pope Leo's *Rerum Novarum*, the solidarists from the passage "capital cannot do without labor nor labor without capital," (no. 19), and distributists from the passage, "The law, therefore, should favor ownership, and its policy should be to induce as many people as possible to become owners" (no. 46). But just as there was no contradiction in the mind of Leo XIII who wrote both these statements, so there is little contradiction in the fundamental thought of Pesch on the one hand, and of Belloc and Chesterton on the other. In

---

3   vol. 1, book 1, p. 18. All references to Pesch are to the translation of the *Lehrbuch* in ten volumes published by Edwin Mellen Press as *Lehrbuch der Nationalökonomie/Teaching Guide to Economics*, c. 2002.

fact, there is a clear convergence with regard to how both systems treat important economic points, such as property or employment and wages.

With reference to property, for example, Pesch wrote of "the need to do away with the individualistic concept of private property,"[4] and that "property is not an end in itself... but it is only a means designed to provide for mankind in a manner appropriate for the well-being of the individual, the family, and political society."[5]

Although the original distributists placed great emphasis on private property and the freedom which property ownership affords to families, the distributist understanding of property is fundamentally the same as that of Pesch. The limits on private property for the sake of the common good which Belloc and Chesterton, as well as contemporary distributists, have championed, presuppose that property ownership is a right only when it is consistent with the common good. Property has a purpose, the support and sustenance of families and individuals, and indirectly of the whole society; it is not a free-standing right to acquire as much as possible with no reference to the common good. Because of this understanding, distributists have suggested a variety of means to break up large concentrations of property, such as Hilaire Belloc's suggestion of using graduated taxation to force the division of large concentrations of property.[6] And of course this is hardly alien to Pesch's thought. There are even passages in Pesch which could have come from the pen of Belloc or Chesterton: "While socialism calls for the abolition of private ownership of the

---

4 vol. 2, bk. 1, p. 264.
5 vol. 1, bk. 1, p. 277.
6 See Belloc's *The Restoration of Property* (New York: Sheed & Ward, [1936] 1946), especially pp. 69–72, 93–118.

means of production, the motto of solidarism is: *increase the number of owners!*"7

Another crucial point where the two systems can be compared is the question of employment and wages. Here Pesch considered that for the most part the employer/employee relationship would continue even in a just economy. He was concerned to insure that workers received a just wage and that owners and workers were bound together in solidarity, both in spirit and in concrete institutions such as occupational groups which were to embody the spirit of justice and charity fundamental to Catholic thought on society. Belloc and Chesterton, for their part, often seemed to speak as if they thought that every worker would become an owner, so that the owner/worker relationship would disappear. But as we saw above, Pesch could go so far as to say that "the motto of solidarism is: *increase the number of owners!*" And on the other hand, Chesterton and Belloc in fact recognized that it was impossible to do away entirely with large entities requiring numerous workers and large capital investments. In *The Outline of Sanity*, when Chesterton wrote about possible means for achieving a distributist economy, he included "the gradual extension of profit-sharing [or] the management of every business . . . by a guild or group. . . . "8 Neither he nor Belloc were absolutists in insisting that every individual or family must own its own farm or small business.

With regard to what is probably the key point in Catholic social teaching, the role of occupational groups, there is likewise considerable overlap between Pesch and the distributists. He wrote,

---

7   Pesch, *Lehrbuch*, vol. 4, book 2, p. 299. Emphasis in original.
8   In *The Collected Works of G. K. Chesterton*, vol. 5, Ignatius Press, 1987, p. 97. Belloc in *The Restoration of Property* makes similar proposals. See p. 88.

Considered overall, solidarism is the social system which brings to proper expression the solidaristic bond among people as such and as members of the natural communities — the family and the state — i.e., in accordance with the specific nature of each community. At the same time it encourages the fullest possible development of cooperative, representative, and corporative associations according to occupation and stations-in-life, as adapted to given historical circumstances, on the firm basis of a community of interests and in a proper juridical form. Considered in the broadest terms possible, the essential meaning of the solidarist system consists in complementing weakness and regulating power by binding people together in solidarity, while exercising mutual consideration and concern in accordance with the demands of justice and charity, by a well-ordered cooperation and reciprocity within the various forms of natural and free, public and private communities, and in accordance with their natural and historical peculiarities, directed toward the ultimate goal of securing the true welfare of everyone involved.[9]

For just as members of a family naturally will cooperate with each other, and just as citizens of the same country will do the same, so those who work in the same firm or industry have common interests and naturally share a common task in the provision of some economic good or service for society. As a result, according to Pesch, the occupational groups will be involved in setting prices, wages, and in many other kinds of economic regulation which today are either done directly by the government, or not at all. Further they would collaborate to solve problems internal to the industry, such as

9   vol. I, book 2, p. 221.

industry-wide collective labor agreements, safety standards and negotiations for contracts with suppliers of raw materials, and with the government and the general public, working both for their own legitimate prosperity and for the public good.

While the central place of occupational groups in continental Catholic social thought, including that of Fr. Pesch, is well-known, less well-known is that they were seen by Belloc and Chesterton as important parts of their own program. In addition to the lines I quoted from Chesterton above, Belloc wrote,

> The safeguarding of the small unit, the seedlings of re-afforestation, the delicate experiments in the reconstruction of property, must take the form of the Guild: not the unprotected guild arising spontaneously (for that would soon be killed by the predatory capitalism around it) but of the Guild *chartered and established by positive law.*[10]

He discusses also the possibility "of chartering . . . trade unions," that is, of conferring official powers on them so they could "regulate wages, consider the opportunities of employment, prevent their function from being swamped with numbers and in general substitute status and order for chaotic competition," as a prelude to setting up formal occupational groups.[11] The reader will see that not only the existence but the functions of such organizations, as conceived by both Pesch and Belloc are similar, and that no one can accuse the distributists of being hostile to the guild-principle.

One can easily see from this that the two major attempts to flesh out the fundamental principles of Catholic social

---

10 *The Restoration of Property*, p. 136. Emphasis in original.
11 *Ibid.*, pp. 139–140.

thought as contained in the papal social encyclicals result in very similar systems. All attempts to do so which take the Church's social doctrine seriously will necessarily exhibit many more similarities than differences and will make clear that social doctrine does have a solid content and that specific proposals can be deduced from it which translate into real world economic policy.

APPENDIX II

RECENT DISCUSSIONS OF
RELIGIOUS LIBERTY

SINCE THE FIRST EDITION OF THIS BOOK appeared in 1998 there has been considerable discussion and debate on *Dignitatis Humanae* in English, Italian, German and other languages. Space and other considerations prevent a thorough review of all this material, which is voluminous, but it is necessary to say something about some of the recent commentary on this question.[12] In the course of doing so I will summarize my argument again with reference to the critique of Professor Thomas Pink and clarify one or two points not covered in chapter two.

Before doing so I remind the reader that despite the unequivocal pledge to maintain traditional Catholic doctrine made at the beginning of *Dignitatis Humanae*, the Declaration does not *seem* to do so. And some at least of its principal framers definitely intended to create new doctrine and apparently thought they had done so. Moreover, they have managed to convince almost everyone else that they had done so too. But it is not the *tone* of the document that we must pay attention to, but "to what the writer succeeded *in setting down on paper explicitly.*"[13] If we can overlook the

12   In the United States in recent years the debate on religious liberty has become part of a larger and more fundamental controversy about the relationship between Catholicism and the classical liberal tradition as a whole.
13   William G. Most, "Religious Liberty: What the Texts Demand," *Faith & Reason*, vol. 9, no. 3, fall 1983, p. 198. Emphasis author's.

rhetoric of *Dignitatis Humanae* and examine its text with care and with correct principles of interpretation, then I think it can be understood in such a way as not to stand in conflict with the earlier teaching.

In an article in the American magazine, *Touchstone*, Korey D. Maas, a Lutheran, summarizes the state of the Catholic debate on religious liberty for an ecumenical readership.[14] Maas notes that

> The Council proceedings made evident the prolonged controversy concerning the discussion of religious liberty, what would become *Dignitatis Humanae* went through nine drafts and hundreds of interventions, with a vote on the text being postponed until the very conclusion of the Council. The greatest source of controversy was quite simply the belief that the document forwarded a doctrine contrary to dogmatic tradition.

Maas continues, "Unsurprisingly, then, the half-century since Vatican II has witnessed a plethora of attempted — but incompatible — clarifications," and he points out the existence of "four distinct positions [that] have been articulated" with regard to how *Dignitatis Humanae* can or cannot be reconciled with previous teaching. The first two simply accept that the Council's teaching was indeed an innovation, "a repudiation of pre-conciliar doctrine." But the two positions regard this very differently. "While agreeing that the Declaration signals a rupture with the dogmatic tradition, 'traditionalists' condemn and 'progressives' celebrate this." The former believe that the Church appears to have repudiated one of her settled teachings, with obviously ominous implications for all of her doctrine, while progressive or liberal Catholics

---

14   "Can We Hang Together?" *Touchstone, A Journal of Mere Christianity*, vol. 31, issue 6, November/December 2018, pp. 52–7.

rejoice because they see the Declaration as opening the door to further, and perhaps widespread, doctrinal change.

The remaining two interpretations of *Dignitatis Humanae* are what Maas calls, first, the neo-conservative view, and secondly, the radical. The first of these upholds the common understanding of *Dignitatis Humanae* as a pretty much unequivocal endorsement of religious liberty, and welcomes this affirmation. But, Maas points out, those who uphold this position differ widely in how they deal with the fact of the previous papal teaching, with some arguing that the apparently new teaching was always implicit in the older texts, while others assert that there are sufficient ambiguities in the teaching of previous pontiffs to allow for doctrinal development, or that the earlier teaching was not "dogmatic in nature [and] merely represented temporary and mutable policy preferences. . . . "

Finally, Maas concludes, the radical view sees the traditional pre-conciliar teaching as authoritative and the Council's Declaration as "ambiguous. If it is to be understood as authoritative, then certain of its interpretations must be corrected to harmonize with the pre-conciliar tradition."

Among those upholding this fourth position, Maas mentions the present writer along with John Lamont, Fr. Thomas Crean and Professor Thomas Pink of King's College, London. It is the latter, however, whose views lately seem to have made considerable headway among those inclined to this kind of solution. I find Professor Pink's attempted explanation unconvincing, however, and I will set forth briefly my objections to it here.

The key point in Pink's method of dealing with the apparent discrepancy between *Dignitatis Humanae* and earlier papal teaching is his claim that the previous doctrine dealt not with the state's inherent right or duty to restrict non-Catholic religious activity for the sake of the common good, but with the Church's right to do so, at least with regard to the baptized. What *Dignitatis Humanae* does, therefore, is to withdraw an earlier authorization given to the civil authorities to restrain or coerce the baptized, on behalf of the Church, but it does not concern the Church's own rights in this area, which remain as before. Thus the Declaration becomes a policy statement, withdrawing a power granted to the state by the Church. But since this grant of authority by the Church to the secular powers was always in principle revocable, *Dignitatis Humanae* does not constitute any change of doctrine, simply a change of policy.

While Professor Pink does well to call attention to the Church's own rights over her subjects — that is, all the baptized — and is correct that this point is often overlooked, this in no way denies that the state may also have certain indirect rights in the religious sphere, insofar as this sphere concerns the preservation of the common good, for in fact it is impossible in practice to separate the temporal good of man entirely from his religious activity. By refocusing the argument exclusively around the Church's rights and authority, Professor Pink has neglected the numerous magisterial passages in which a certain authority to safeguard and promote Catholic practice and to restrict non-Catholic religious conduct is seen as proper to the state's own duties and rights.

Professor Pink has drawn from his studies on earlier Catholic thinkers, particularly Suárez and Bellarmine, to support his thesis. But whatever positions those earlier thinkers took on this matter, and no matter how much any of their writings may have been esteemed by any of the sovereign pontiffs, or even "commissioned by" any of them,[15] still such writings

---

15 Professor Pink speaks of Suárez's work, *Defensio Fidei Catholicae* as being "commissioned by Paul V and directed against James I of England." Thomas Pink, "Conscience and Coercion," *First Things*,

are not part of the Church's magisterial teaching, and even if they do reflect the thinking of any particular pope, that does not make them part of the Church's doctrine.[16] Lastly, if Professor Pink wishes to confine the power of dealing with religious matters solely to the Church, with the state's authority in this area seen merely as something granted by the Church, it is not clear how he can explain the rights of the state to regulate religious activity on the part of unbaptized persons, over whom the Church has no rights whatsoever. Let us look at each of these points in order.

It seems clear from Pope Leo's oft repeated assertions of the state's duty toward the true Faith that he did teach that the state itself has a certain care for the religious life of its citizens, inasmuch as this affects the common good. This is not a mere grant of authority by which the state acts on behalf of the Church. I think that any common-sense interpretation of the following quotations from Leo's encyclicals will bear out this claim.

> So, too, is it a sin in the State not to have care for religion, as a something beyond its scope, or as of no practical benefit; or out of many forms of religion to adopt that one which chimes in with the fancy; for we are bound absolutely to worship God in that way which He has shown to be His will. All who rule, therefore, should hold in honor the

---

August/September 2012, pp. 46–7.

16 We might compare such endorsements with the praise that Pope Benedict XV gave to Fr. Augustine Roesler's World War I era book, *Die Frauenfrage*, which the Pope described as "a book . . . in which [readers] might safely and thoroughly and clearly discover what they should think of the social position of women according to the laws of the Catholic religion." (Quoted in William B. Faherty, *The Destiny of Modern Woman in the Light of Papal Teaching*, Westminster: Newman Press, 1950, p. 63.) Yet no one today would consider a Catholic as bound by Fr. Roesler's opinions on the civil status or social role of women.

holy name of God, and one of their chief duties
must be to favor religion, to protect it, to shield
it under the credit and sanction of the laws, and
neither to organize nor enact any measure that may
compromise its safety. This is the bounden duty of
rulers to the people over whom they rule.

—*Immortale Dei*, no. 6.

But, to justify [liberty of worship], it must needs
be taken as true that the State has no duties toward
God, or that such duties, if they exist, can be aban-
doned with impunity, both of which assertions
are manifestly false. For it cannot be doubted but
that, by the will of God, men are united in civil
society; whether its component parts be considered; or its form, which implies authority; or the
object of its existence; or the abundance of the
vast services which it renders to man. God it is
who has made man for society, and has placed
him in the company of others like himself, so that
what was wanting to his nature, and beyond his
attainment if left to his own resources, he might
obtain by association with others. Wherefore, civil
society must acknowledge God as its Founder and
Parent, and must obey and reverence His power
and authority. Justice therefore forbids, and reason itself forbids, the State to be godless; or to
adopt a line of action which would end in godlessness—namely, to treat the various religions (as
they call them) alike, and to bestow upon them
promiscuously equal rights and privileges. Since,
then, the profession of one religion is necessary in
the State, that religion must be professed which
alone is true, and which can be recognized without
difficulty, especially in Catholic states....

—*Libertas*, no. 21

Men have a right freely and prudently to propagate throughout the State what things soever are true and honorable, so that as many as possible may possess them; but lying opinions, than which no mental plague is greater, and vices which corrupt the heart and moral life, should be diligently repressed by public authority, lest they insidiously work the ruin of the State.

— *Libertas*, no. 23.

[T]he more a State is driven to tolerate evil, the further is it from perfection; and that the tolerance of evil which is dictated by political prudence should be strictly confined to the limits which its justifying cause, the public welfare, requires.

— *Libertas*, no. 34

Professor Pink quotes *Immortale Dei*, that "it is the Church, and not the State, that is to be man's guide to heaven" (no. 11), and "Whatever, therefore, in things human is of a sacred character, whatever belongs . . . to the salvation of souls or to the worship of God, is subject to the power and judgment of the Church" (no. 13). But in view of the quotations from Leo that are set out immediately above, it seems clear that the sweeping conclusion that he draws from these quotations is not justified, namely, that "according to Leo XIII, in matters of religion the Church is the only authority with the right to coerce."[17] Moreover, even without reference to the Leonine statements about the state's duties in this area, the attentive reader will see that Leo is not saying anything regarding state coercion or authority in religious matters in the two quotes from *Immortale Dei* that Professor Pink adduces. Rather, Leo is pointing out that it is the Church's task to lead us to heaven, and that her internal

---

17 Pink, "Conscience and Coercion," p. 47.

affairs — her worship and teaching, for example — are solely her concern, not the state's. Moreover, we should recall that in the discussion of the state's rights to regulate religious activity on behalf of the common good, we are looking solely at the activity of non-Catholics, to whom no divine mandate has been given to care for the religious life of mankind at all, and whom therefore the two passages from *Immortale Dei* which Professor Pink quotes do not concern at all.

In addition to those passages which I have quoted, there is one more which it seems necessary to mention, the address of Pius XII, *Ci Riesce*, to the Union of Italian Catholic Jurists of December 6, 1953. Speaking of the authority of the state, Pius asks,

> Could it be that *in certain circumstances* [God] would not give men any mandate, would not impose any duty, and would not even communicate the right to impede or to repress what is erroneous and false? A look at things as they are gives an affirmative answer. (no. 17).

The Pope is speaking here of political authority, as the whole address makes clear, and the point of the discussion is whether at times God might not "communicate the right to impede or to repress what is erroneous and false." It is simply assumed here that at times God *does* communicate such a right, and nowhere in the text is there the slightest suggestion that this is a matter of a grant of authority on the part of the Church. In fact, a few paragraphs later, Pius XII states that it is "the Catholic statesman [who] must judge if this condition [calling for toleration] is verified in the concrete," although he also notes that such a statesman will seek the "guidance," but, note, not the *permission*, of the Church in making such a decision on behalf of the toleration of what is objectively evil.

Since Pius XII speaks of occasions when God might "not even communicate the right to impede or to repress what is erroneous and false," obviously this cannot be a reference to the rights of the Church in this area, for the authority which the Church possesses over her own subjects is not something which is granted by God only according to circumstances, but is always present.

Then, with regard to unbaptized persons, Professor Pink asserts the Church's right to some authority over them.

> But the Church still has the authority to use coercion to defend her jurisdiction against those unbaptized who interfere from without, proselytizing on behalf of false religions.[18]

He provides no text to support this view, however. While it is certainly the case that the state was traditionally seen as having such powers over its unbaptized citizens, as part of the state's care of the common good, it is hard to see how such a right could belong to the Church herself, and hence be delegated by the Church to the state.

Finally, Professor Pink asserts that *Dignitatis Humanae* absolutely forbids state intrusion into the religious realm.

> [B]ecause the good of religion does altogether transcend the authority of the state, our right not to be coerced by the state where the good of religion alone is at stake admits of no exceptions. The state cannot restrict our liberty for specifically religious ends, to protect religious truth, or simply for people's religious good.[19]

---

18 Pink, "Conscience and Coercion," p. 47.
19 Thomas Pink, "*Dignitatis Humanae*: continuity after Leo XIII," Available on academia.edu, p. 1.

But in fact *Dignitatis Humanae* is not so absolute in its teaching as Pink maintains. In addition to the well-known exceptions based on "due limits" and the "just requirements of public order" (no. 2) there is the far more important but often neglected statement in no. 7 that "the common good of all" is one of the factors to be taken into account with regard to the state's care of religious conduct. In fact it was the common good that was traditionally seen as the chief factor that ought to guide the civil authorities in their legislation on religious matters.

Of course the state authorities do not exercise their powers in a vacuum. Catholic rulers must learn their religion from the Church, just as anyone else. But the authority that they hold for the sake of the common good to regulate the public religious activity of non-Catholics, and to protect and promote the Catholic faith, is not based on a grant of authority given by the Church, but is part of the "bounden duty of rulers to the people over whom they rule."

Professor Pink also quotes a number of the *relationes* or official explanations of the meaning of *Dignitatis Humanae* given to the Council Fathers during their deliberations on the text, and claims that these explanations support his interpretation of what the Council was doing.[20] He points out that they emphasize the fact that *Dignitatis Humanae* concerns only religious freedom in the civil order, and not in the Church. This, he argues, confirms his position that the Council's Declaration was merely the withdrawal of a prior permission granted to the state to enforce the Church's rights over her own baptized subjects. But I think that this is an anachronistic reading of these statements. During and after the Council there was discussion of whether or how

---

20 Thomas Pink, "*Dignitatis Humanae*: continuity after Leo XIII," pp. 15ff.

far the (presumed) teaching of *Dignitatis Humanae* might affect the freedom of a Catholic *vis-à-vis* the Church. Thus John Courtney Murray, in his introduction to *Dignitatis Humanae* for the Abbott edition of the Council's documents, wrote,

> [T]hough the Declaration deals only with the minor issue of religious freedom in the technical secular sense, it does affirm a principle of wider import — that the dignity of man consists in his responsible use of freedom. Some of the conciliar Fathers — not least those opposed to the Declaration — perceived that a certain indivisibility attaches to the notion of freedom... The conciliar affirmation of the principle of freedom was narrowly limited — in the text. But the text itself was flung into a pool whose shores are wide as the universal Church. The ripples will run far.
>
> Inevitably, a second great argument will be set afoot.... The children of God ... assert it within the Church as well as in the world.... [21]

Although Fr. Murray's remarks do concern the Church's rights and authority over her members, they do so not in the sense that Professor Pink believes. That is, they are not concerned with a grant of power to the civil authorities, but with questions such as whether a Catholic has a right to dissent from Church teaching, for example. No one at the time raised the question of the state acting as agent for the Church to coerce its citizens in religious matters. [22]

---

21 Walter Abbott, ed., *The Documents of Vatican II*, pp. 673–4.
22 See, for example, the address to the Council of Bishop Emile De Smedt on November 19, 1963, introducing the draft on religious liberty, which at the time was still a part of the ecumenical schema. (Vatican Council II, *Acta Synodalia*, vol. II, periodus 2, pars V, pp. 485–95. Reprinted and translated in *Council Daybook, Vatican II, Session 1*,

Shortly before *Dignitatis Humanae* was given final approval, on September 15, 1965, John Courtney Murray gave an address at the Dutch Documentation Center in Rome on the pending religious liberty schema. Nowhere in his speech is there the slightest hint of the meaning of the text that Professor Pink advocates. Fr. Murray reviews the teaching of Leo XIII, focusing exclusively on Leo's conception of the state and its rulers, and whether they possess a *patria potestas* over their subjects, etc. But no reference to what Professor Pink claims was the point at issue.[23]

Before concluding I will deal briefly with Professor Pink's comments on my own and similar positions.[24]. He writes,

> It is . . . remarkable that so many authors attempt to reconcile *Dignitatis Humanae* with the pre-conciliar magisterium by appealing to the just public order exception. These authors claim that in the Catholic societies of the past, non-Catholic religious activity and proselytization in the public sphere . . . did once threaten just public order as it might not be threatened now, and then suggest that the Catholic magisterium was calling on the state to restrict such activity just on that account.

Professor Pink then quotes me to the effect that

> "just requirements of public order," the "due limits," and considerations of the rights of others and of the common good vary considerably from society

---

Session 2, edited by Floyd Anderson, Washington: National Catholic Welfare Conference, 1965, pp. 277–82.)
23 Reprinted in *Council Daybook, Vatican II, Session 4*, edited by Floyd Anderson, Washington: National Catholic Welfare Conference, 1966, pp. 14–17.
24 Thomas Pink, "*Dignitatis Humanae*: continuity after Leo XIII." Quotes are from pp. 3ff.

to society, and in a society overwhelmingly and traditionally Catholic they could easily include restrictions, and even an outright prohibition, on the public activities of non-Catholic sects, particularly their proselytizing activities.

Professor Pink responds to the position of myself and of other authors holding similar views, as follows,

> But this is to misunderstand the Church's past conception of the state's role when privileging Catholicism — which was primarily to protect the spiritual good of its citizens, and not simply to protect just public order under civil and social conditions very different from those of the present. The state's coercive role was to protect the Church and her mission as essential to the supreme spiritual good of salvation, and not just to protect the civil order.

I find this comment odd, for I do not understand how "the spiritual good of its citizens" can be separated from "public order," and especially from "the common good of all." As I said above, it is impossible to separate the temporal good of mankind — which is directly under the care of the state — from our eternal destiny, for the two are interwoven, as this entire book illustrates again and again.

Moreover, the fact that "previous teaching justified not only restrictions on the public activity of false religions, but also coercing heretics to return to the true faith" is not at issue here, as the latter was clearly a power of the Church, and insofar as the Church sought the support of the state in implementing it, this was indeed an example of the Church asking the assistance of the civil powers, and in effect, delegating a certain authority to them. The fact that the Church's powers over heretics are more far-reaching than those possessed by the state does not mean that the state has no duties of its own in the religious sphere, however.

To sum up my argument, then: Man has a right, in the political order, to religious freedom.[25] This is affirmed by *Dignitatis Humanae*, and in the context of that Declaration this assertion might seem to be at variance with the earlier teaching. But this is not really the case. For, as *Dignitatis Humanae* itself asserts in no. 7, the exercise of this freedom is limited by the concerns of the common good, a teaching reaffirmed by the *Catechism of the Catholic Church* (nos. 1738 and 2109). Thus, since the common good differs from one social situation to another, as the *Catechism* also points out (no. 2109), the degree of religious liberty rightly permitted to non-Catholics differs from one social situation to another. In overwhelmingly and traditional Catholic societies, we may rightly see public non-Catholic religious activity, especially proselytizing, as contrary to the common good, though non-Catholics would still enjoy their right to the *private* exercise of their religion, above all in their own homes. Thus non-Catholics would always enjoy a political right to religious liberty, but the "due limits" which a state must place on this right "must be determined for each social situation by political prudence, according to the requirements of the common good...," as the *Catechism* teaches.[26]

The foundation of the de facto practice of allowing non-Catholics private religious liberty was not altogether clear in the earlier teaching. Did they have any kind of right to such liberty or was it merely something tolerated for the sake of the common good and the peace of the society as a whole? But while this aspect of the teaching was undeveloped, the

---

25   Clearly there can be no *moral* right to embrace error, only a *political* right to be free of external restraint on the part of the state.
26   No. 2109.

relevant pre-Vatican II papal documents never excluded the notion of a right of religious liberty for non-Catholics in certain circumstances. For example, in the *Syllabus of Errors* (no. 78), Pius IX condemned the "public exercise" of non-Catholic religions in Catholic states. And as I quoted above, in *Ci Riesce*, Pius XII says that God "would not even communicate the right" to restrict non-Catholic religious activity in some circumstances. Thus I do not think it is contradictory to say that there could be a right (in the political order) to religious liberty for non-Catholics, the exercise of which right, like all others, is subject to the exigencies of the common good. Thus non-Catholics would always have a right to *private* religious activity, and where they are a majority or a large or traditional minority or otherwise where the common good indicates, they also have a right to at least some public religious freedom. But, on the other hand, in Catholic nations the common good would usually indicate limitation, at least to some extent, of their public religious acts. This position, I think, is perfectly consistent both with the earlier teaching and with *Dignitatis Humanae*. It is true that *Dignitatis Humanae* emphasizes the right to religious freedom, but it contains sufficient in the way of limitations to make it compatible with that "traditional Catholic teaching" it undertook to develop, while at the same time, like all true doctrinal development, leaving what came before "intact." Thus *Dignitatis Humanae*'s contribution to the development of doctrine may be seen to lie in its giving the religious liberty of non-Catholics a firmer theological foundation, i.e., pointing out that their liberty is likewise founded on *right*. But note that their religious liberty is not the same as the exercise of that liberty, which is limited by the requirements of the common good, as *Dignitatis Humanae* itself clearly states in no. 7.